P9-CAS-443

the new color of SUCCESS

the new color

Twenty Young Black Millionaire

Niki Butler Mitchell

of SUCCESS

Tell You How They're Making It

PRIMA PUBLISHING

*To my husband, Daryl, who is patient, kind, and
loving and who literally made this book possible and
my dream of being a writer come true.
And to Mom and Dad, who believed in me
when no one else did.*

© 1999 by Adler & Robin Books, Inc.

All rights reserved. No part of this book may be reproduced or transmitted in any form or by any means, electronic or mechanical, including photocopying, recording, or by any information storage or retrieval system, without written permission from Prima Publishing, except for the inclusion of quotations in a review.

All products mentioned in this book are trademarks of their respective companies.

Prima Publishing and colophon are registered trademarks of Prima Communications, Inc.

Library of Congress Cataloging-in-Publication Data
Mitchell, Niki Butler.
    The new color of success: twenty young black millionaires
tell you how they're making it / Niki Butler Mitchell.
        p.   cm.
Includes bibliographical references and index.
ISBN 0-7615-2065-1
    1. Wealth—United States.   2. Millionaires—United States.   3. Afro-American businesspeople—Interviews.   4. Success in business—United States—Case studies.   I. Title: Twenty young black millionaires tell you how they're making it.   II. Title.

HC110.W4 M57 2000
650.1'089'96073—dc21
                                                                                        99-049381

99 00 01 HH 10 9 8 7 6 5 4 3 2 1

Printed in the United States of America

How to Order
Single copies may be ordered from Prima Publishing, P.O. Box 1260BK, Rocklin, CA 95677; telephone (916) 632-4400. Quantity discounts are also available. On your letterhead, include information concerning the intended use of the books and the number of books you wish to purchase.

Visit us online at www.primalifestyles.com

Contents

CHAPTER 20: 1   , PA

EBON I. HUGHES CEO
EBON ENGINEERING

I AM A GREAT believer in and proponent of the philosophy that the African American community will begin to fully realize the promises of this nation when it recognizes that economic empowerment and the enlightened use of political will are the keys to leveraging change for the good of the entire black community.

Business is the means to that power, and the stories in *The New Color of Success* exemplify some of this country's best up-and-coming stars of the age-old entrepreneurial tradition in the African American community. African Americans have a long and illustrious history as innovators and business owners in a vast variety of fields, and many of their stories have been told in the pages of *Black Enterprise* magazine. Yet this history is often obscured by the images and perceptions we live with daily. When I started *Black Enterprise* magazine nearly thirty years ago, advertisers were reluctant to believe that there was actually a black middle class out there worth courting. We had to and still have to convince advertisers that the black consumer market has an interest in stocks, bonds, and other financial instruments, that this market does indeed buy luxury cars and computers, and that yes, many of us own our own businesses.

We must fight constantly to reaffirm the validity of the black consumer market because the vision of it shared by some large corporations is limited to the inner city and low-income housing. Alternatively, the handful of successful African Americans who gain widespread attention are sports figures and entertainers, which fuels the perception that when we do succeed, we only do so on stage or on the court.

The value of Niki Mitchell's enlightening book is that it dispels that notion and exposes the larger public to another side of the black community, bringing young African American entrepreneurs from behind the curtain of invisibility and into the light. By doing so, it accomplishes the feat of educating what I hope will be large multi-racial readership about the talent we have always known exists in our community, while providing role models and inspiration for everyone, especially young African Americans who dream of owning a business one day.

Almost three years ago, I published a book about black entrepreneurship entitled *How To Succeed in Business Without Being White*, in which I detailed what it takes to make it as a business owner. More recently, Black Enterprise Books introduced *Titans of the B.E. 100s*, profiling CEOs who have been the vanguard of the entrepreneurial revolution in the African American community. The people featured in these books are the living, breathing embodiment of the traits I believe are critical for success. They are tenacious, thoughtful risk takers, flexible, solution-focused, energetic and always on the lookout for future opportunities. The new generation of entrepreneurs as profiled in *The New Color of Success* are following suit and are all the more admirable because they have a more difficult road to walk than I and my peers had thirty years ago.

When I started in business there was an awakening in white America inspired by the loud and righteous demands for equality defined by the civil rights movement. Laws protecting civil rights had been hammered out, sometimes in blood, and the white establishment seemed to recognize that it was easier and more cost-efficient to provide opportunity to 12 percent of the population than to deny it. That worked to my advantage in the early days of black enterprise as it did for other African Americans seeking a foothold.

The challenges were formidable in 1970, but compared to the racial climate today, it was harmony and brotherhood back then. I have said before that we were pioneers then. We are warriors today. The social, political, and business environments today are far more hostile than they were thirty years ago. Words such as *preferential* and *progressive* bring scorn and bitterness from the mouths of congressional and business leaders as well as talk radio demagogues. Affirmative action, which greatly accelerated the creation and growth of the black professional class and spurred economic development throughout this country, now is wrongly blamed for everything from corporate downsizing to the lowering of educational standards in schools. The noble and inherently fair idea of providing opportunity for those from whom it has been denied is now strapped to the whipping post and regularly flayed by those who remain hostile to our ambitions.

Each of these stories demonstrate that young African Americans recognize and are unbowed before the challenges they face in a world where racism has reemerged as a pervasive and reenergized force. They are fighting the good fight with courage and grace, knowing they can take nothing for granted, knowing they have to be stronger, smarter, and work longer and harder than their white counterparts. They must continue to convince the corporate world that doing business with black America is not a charitable deed—it simply makes good business sense. They have realized too that *carpe diem* is not just a slogan but a battle cry: We must seize the day if we are to affect, individually and collectively, true change in this country. Now more than ever, African Americans are searching for more and greater entrepreneurial opportunities. Today, black economic empowerment—black wealth—is the primary weapon in the fight for true freedom and equality. We have made great progress, and if the people profiled in *The New Color of Success* are any indication, we are well on our way to even greater heights.

—EARL G. GRAVES
Chairman and CEO of Earl G. Graves Ltd.
Founder, editor, and publisher of *Black Enterprise* magazine

Introduction

WHEN I FIRST told people that I was writing a book about young black millionaires, I was surprised at the responses I got, mostly because there was a common presumption that they already knew who would be in the book. "That's a great idea. Are they rappers? Singers? Basketball players?" Or, "Will Oprah be in the book? She's rich." When I explained that the book was about millionaires who were entrepreneurs in a variety of fields that did not call on hip-hop skills or anything related to a ball, I was met with blank looks, from blacks and whites alike. It was as if the thought that black people could prosper at anything other than entertainment and sports was outside the normal range of comprehension. One person struggled valiantly with the idea of black entrepreneurs and finally suggested that he knew someone who had made money owning a chicken franchise. Well, the franchise guy is not in this book, either.

I decided to write this book to tell stories that are rarely told. When researching this book I ran across a quote from an observer who said that in the white community the role model is a businessman, while in the black community you've got 26 million folks trying to be 200 athletes and 300 entertainers. He is absolutely right. The larger society is notorious for its iconolatry of the physical and the beautiful: sports stars, singers, actors, models. But business leaders are almost as idolized. Donald Trump, Bill Gates and Michael Milken are household names.

Yet in the black community, virtually all we see and know are who plays ball and who's singing what, with a few exceptions (think Colin Powell or Jesse Jackson). Every person in America knows Michael Jordan, Tiger Woods, Oprah Winfrey, and Whitney Houston, but I would bet my house that two out of three people on the street cannot name the president and chief operating officer of American Express (African American Kenneth I. Chenault, who assumes the position of CEO in 2001).

Part of the fault lies with the black community. We have failed to educate ourselves and our children about our entrepreneurial history, about black business leaders of yesterday and today, and about the endless possibilities entrepreneurship represents for economic self-sufficiency and freedom. Most of us are so busy chasing a paycheck that we never stop to think about our employment options; many of us do not even know what options exist.

What It Takes

IF these stories prove anything, it is that, as John Bryant (chapter 2) so eloquently put it, success is simply the ability to outrun failure. For every one of these millionaire business owners (and the up and comers standing in the wings), success came as a result of dogged pursuit, of steely persistence, or of plain stubbornness. Some plotted their business rise step-by-step. Others started businesses without a clue about where they were going or how they would get there. Some did it without college degrees and without extensive knowledge of business principles. They all learned on the job. Most of the folks whose stories I chronicle fell numerous times, only to get back up, dust off, and re-enter the race.

Folks with day jobs often look at business owners as mythic and lucky figures who have some secret knowledge about how to achieve professional independence and wealth. But the overarching lesson here is that there is no set formula or special mix of prerequisites required for business success. You don't have to inherit a fortune, go to the Harvard Business School, or be a certifiable genius to start and run a successful business.

You do need a dream, a plan, and perseverance. You need to learn from your mistakes. You need the will to keep slogging forward when it seems hopeless.

The Sound of Silence

THE people in this book are examples of the above-mentioned principles, yet their business success stories as a phenomenon have gone largely unnoticed by mainstream media. This in spite of the fact that, according to the Small Business Administration, in 1997, there were 881,646 black-owned businesses, a 108 percent increase since 1987. In addition, black entrepreneurs in some areas are starting businesses at nearly twice the rate of other business owners.

The media "blackout" extends to books as well and seems to prove that blacks are still subject to the Invisible Man syndrome forty years after Ralph Ellison made the observation in his groundbreaking novel. The runaway bestseller *The Millionaire Next Door,* which took pains to detail and study wealth accumulation by ancestry group and included Latvians, Estonians and Luxembourgers, excluded African Americans. Perhaps the omission was due to the methodology used to find the millionaires surveyed. But the exclusion of African Americans from a widely read book lauding industriousness and economic productivity by ancestral group suggests by implication two things: (1) that African Americans are less industrious than other groups and (2) that African Americans have the advantage of a level playing field. Neither is true.

The Black Millionaire Next Door

AS this book demonstrates, black entrepreneur millionaires are found in every profession: telecommunications, Internet services, wine distribution, media management, helicopter tours, public relations, and toxic cleanup, to name only a few covered here. In fact, there is a long tradition of entrepreneurship in the African American community, dating back to the arrival of the slaves on these shores. According to John Sibley Butler, author of the scholarly work *Entrepreneurship and Self-Help Among Black Americans: A Reconsideration of Race and Economics*, slaves often ran their owners' businesses, a phenomenon described as *intrapraneurship*. And there are numerous examples of blacks succeeding in business after the end of slavery. For instance, Robert Gordon managed his master's coal yard and was allowed to keep the profits from the sale of coal leavings. He bought his freedom in 1846 and founded his own successful coal yard. He retired in 1885 a rich man.

The stories in this book are a testament to the African American heritage of entrepreneurship, which today is sometimes carried on against all odds. For example, Robin Petgrave's (chapter 4) $4 million flight training school and helicopter tour service began with $300 and a telephone. A multimillion-dollar advertising and publicity firm was started by thirty-year-old Sibrena Stowe (chapter 18), who moved to New York with only $1,000, a daughter, and a dream. These and the other stories of the journey to success will inspire anyone who works hard every day and dreams of starting his or her own business— maybe even becoming a millionaire. They are classic American success stories, made all the more impressive because the individuals profiled have had more obstacles to overcome than their white counterparts, not the least of which is doubt from others about their abilities.

Who Are They?

THIS talented group was chosen on the basis of the worth of their businesses, not what they have in their personal bank accounts. My point was to find people who were more interested in building a piece of the future, in black wealth and economic empowerment, than in accumulating possessions. Every person in this small cross-section of black entrepreneurs is more interested in making money than spending it. That is an important distinction, given that social critics have long decried the tendency of black Americans—who represent close to $500 billion dollars in buying power, or the equivalent of the world's ninth largest market—to squander our economic power instead of leveraging it for the political benefit of the black community. The folks in these pages understand the difference between a nice income and building wealth: An income is money to spend; building wealth requires an investment in a business, stocks, or some other method of making money work for you as opposed to simply working for money.

Many of the individuals I interviewed did not finish college, but they often tout the value of education. Regardless of education, they are some of the smartest, most courageous, and persistent people you could ever meet. None had an early identifiable or defining talent, meaning no one picked up a golf club or a microphone at age two and thus sealed their fate as the next Tiger Woods or Mariah Carey. Most inherited nothing from their families but a willingness to work hard, think big, and dream of possibilities without limitations. Perhaps it is a delayed legacy of the civil rights movement, but this new generation of entrepreneurs seems bolder, defined by confidence and lack of fear: They refuse to be told what they cannot do, where they cannot go, what they cannot achieve. Renewed attacks on civil rights laws, unequal access to educational and economic opportunities, and the growing hostility to affirmative action do not deter them.

A prevailing characteristic among those profiled here is what might have been labeled as "uppity" in the not-so-distant past. Things have indeed changed since Martin Luther King, Jr., raised that glorious ruckus forty years ago. One new development seems to be a sense of entitlement among young black folks. We've been integrated just enough to recognize what we could have, and a few of us just decided to go get it.

The proprietors of Mojo Highway, for instance, two of the country's first African American brewers (chapter 15), chose to make beer because they like it and it's what they want to do. Going into the venture, it never occurred to them on any conscious level that they were making history.

Myra Peterson (chapter 5) is the creator of Urbanrepublic.com, the first "cybermall" with high-quality products, services, and information targeted to African Americans.

Every one of the young entrepreneurs in this book had a support network—whether family, friends, peers, professors, or professional mentors—but the external support would not have helped without the strong self-esteem that is another characteristic these bold businesspeople share. It is why Deborah Sawyer (chapter 10), now president of her own environmental consulting and services firm, majored in science even though college counselors who had doubts about a black woman's ability to undertake college-level science and math courses tried to steer her away from hard science. Self-esteem is why John Bryant (chapter 2) responded to an advisor who told him he was "too dumb to fail" by becoming such a smart investment broker that he got bankers to do the impossible: invest in South Central Los Angeles after riots left much of it a smoldering pile of rubble.

Finally, everyone in this book has contributed to a legacy of entrepreneurship for the next generation, and they share something else as well: passion. If you love what you do, it becomes easier to wake up in the morning, to work long hours, and to take great risks. It is my hope that this book unlocks the mystery for some who need a little inspiration to get up off the couch (or out of a dead-end job) and stalk a dream. And for the young brothers and sisters out there who are just starting out in business, I hope these chapters challenge you to realize your dream.

Acknowledgments

SEVERAL EXTRAORDINARY WRITER friends contributed to this book and served as critics, editors, taskmasters, cheerleaders, and bullies when needed. They are Michelle Collison, Cheryl Fields, Amy Bowles Reyer, Karen Hirsch, and TaRessa Stovall, who actually was my writing collaborator on some of the book. Thank you, and I love you all.

People in general have been extremely helpful and supportive of this effort. I often called friends of friends without even a formal introduction, and when they understood what the project was about they helped enthusiastically with referrals, leads on prospective interviews, advice, and feedback. They are Lalohni Alsobrook, Vince Mickens, Dwight Mims, Dwight Langhum, Sherry Tiggett, David Fishlow, Andre Suite, Tama Smith, Greg Roberts, Joe Pryor, and Charlene Meeks, among others.

I also thank my literary agent, Djana Pearson Morris, whose idea this was in the first place, Susan Silva, my editor at Prima Publishing, and everyone on the editing and publicity team who had faith in this project and put great effort into its realization. I also thank everybody who agreed to be interviewed for the book. They were, with rare exceptions, wonderfully open about their experiences and trials.

And finally, I thank my family and my friends, including Bill, who stay positive no matter what and who make believing in the unthinkable entirely reasonable.

CHAPTER 1

A New Day

Yvette Lee Bowser
President and CEO
SisterLee Productions
Hollywood, California

Founded: 1992
Number of Employees: 150
Initial Investment: $0

YVETTE LEE BOWSER is a little like the Rosa Parks of television. The civil rights icon launched a revolution by refusing to budge from her seat on an Alabama bus. Ms. Parks was just tired, but that simple act of defiance set in motion a social change of enormous magnitude. Yvette was also tired—tired of the typical, one-dimensional depictions of black women in film and on prime-time television: faithful slave, tragic mulatto, sassy mama.

Out of the desire to see more realistic portrayals of black women, Yvette Lee Bowser not only became the first African American woman to produce a successful prime-time series, the hit television comedy *Living Single,* but also stood her ground and won the right to produce it largely as she envisioned it: a show about six friends—four professional African American women and two men—who are independent, intelligent, successful, educated, and funny. Finally, a show centered around African American women who are living life on their terms—not a neck-working, butt-shaking, welfare-dependent Sapphire in the lot.

Given that popular media has a strong impact on perceptions of race, Yvette helped shape a revolution in the image of African Americans. As Yvette explained in *African-American Screenwriters Now,* her goal was "to produce a positive, hilarious show about young African Americans trying to make it. It's important to me that the show came from a positive place and that it depicts us loving each other in our own way." As the first ensemble comedy about the platonic relationships among a group of men and women, *Living Single* was the archetypal predecessor of the NBC sitcom *Friends.* The show was also a giant step forward for womankind. For once, landing a man was not the central and only focus of the characters' lives. Speaking of her groundbreaking role, Yvette states, "I want to leave a legacy of positive images because I really believe in karma. I believe that the deeds you do come back to you."

Yvette's refusal to compromise her integrity, or that of the show or its characters, proved prescient. *Living Single,* which debuted on the FOX television network in August 1993, quickly became the number-one show among African American viewers and remained number one for its entire five-year run. The show helped establish FOX as a contender in the competition for ratings and thus a network to be taken seriously.

Running the Show

THE powerhouse behind her own highly successful production company, SisterLee Productions, Yvette is already, at the tender age of thirty-three, a television veteran and currently both writer and executive producer (in association with Warner Brothers) of her latest sitcom creation, *For Your Love.* Now in its third broadcast season on the Warner Brothers network (WB), *For Your Love* is the third prime-time sitcom Yvette Lee Bowser has created and produced for television. This places her in a very small and exclusive club of African Americans who run shows—other members include Bill Cosby, Susan Fales, producer of *A Different World,* and Benny Medina, producer of *The Fresh Prince of Bel-Air.*

> *"It's a new day, and opportunities are there for those who are willing to work. Just be prepared for a lot of rejection."*

Yvette now manages 150 people, including crew, office personnel, and a staff of writers. SisterLee recently signed a three-year deal with Warner Brothers and has numerous projects in the works, proof that there are opportunities out there for young African Americans who want to follow the rarely trod path of television sitcom writer and producer. The good news is that it can be done. The less good news is that Hollywood is a tough nut to crack but, as Yvette puts it, "It's a new day, and opportunities are there for those who are willing to work. Just be prepared for a lot of rejection."

SisterLee is on a mission to diversify and heighten television standards as they pertain to African Americans, other people of color, and women. It is a formidable endeavor. Forward movement and change—whether it is changing minds or images—tend to progress slowly. But Yvette believes that she has achieved a degree of success because "they haven't put me out yet," though executives sometimes sigh when they see her coming, carrying that political agenda.

> *I am constantly being challenged to educate people about what is racist, what is sexist, and what is just plain not amusing."*

Able to swim the shark-infested waters of television with grace and wit, Yvette is wise beyond her years, a survivor in a world as Machiavellian and political as Washington. Perhaps part of her charm and one of her survival mechanisms is that she has a talent for disarming irony. Asked about her greatest challenge, her answer is: "I am constantly being challenged to educate people about what is racist, what is sexist, and what is just plain not amusing. At a certain point in life, people should know that to refer to a woman's breasts as 'the twins' is just not amusing."

In the Beginning

YVETTE Lee Bowser started at the bottom. At the age of twenty-two, two months out of Stanford with a shiny new dual degree in political science and psychology and every intention of attending law school, Yvette changed her mind and decided to become a writer. It happened "on a whim," she reports.

Yvette had been writing all her life: She wrote plays for show-and-tell, she wrote short stories, she worked for the newspaper in high school. But there is an invisible line between "writing" and "being a writer." "Writing" is a hobby. "Being a writer" suggests soul-deep commitment. Yvette did not make the leap from one side of the divide to the other until she was faced with one of those life-defining choices often foreshadowed by a completely unremarkable event. As she sat watching television with a friend one night, generally lamenting the state of post-college life, she recognized the name of an acquaintance among the credits of *The Cosby Show* on NBC. She gave the friend a call, one thing led to another, and eventually Yvette got to meet with Mr. Cosby himself. Though he expressed admiration for her short stories and budding talent, he was less than encouraging. "He told me, 'There's nothing out here for you. Go to law school,'" Yvette recalls.

Cosby even found a couple to fund her entire law school education. Yvette could have afforded law school with the usual loans and grants, but the offer of a free education with no strings attached was like an offer from the gods. It was an agonizing decision, but, facing the fact that she was no longer interested in becoming a member of the bar and wanted to pursue a career in television instead, Yvette declined the generous offer.

Having once made up her mind, Yvette was steel in her resolve. "I said, 'I'll get coffee, I'll get sandwiches, I'll do whatever it takes,'" she remembers. "I passed up the opportunity of a lifetime to work in Hollywood. I was determined to do something creative."

Persistence won out. Yvette finally managed to persuade Bill Cosby to give her a job as a writer's apprentice on *A Different World,* a *Cosby Show* spin-off about life at a historically black college. Yvette indeed got coffee and sandwiches, but she also got an invaluable look at how television is created and even made story contributions. As a recent college graduate, she was close in age and experience to the show's characters, and soon her ideas were appearing in the plot lines and dialogue with such regularity that she recalls thinking, "Maybe I should call Mr. Cosby to see if I should be getting paid for this."

On-the-Job Training

YVETTE's apprentice pay started out at $200 a week, but the opportunity proved to be priceless. Within four years, her drive, ambition, and innate writing ability won her a coveted spot as a co-producer. In the fifth season, promoted to producer, she was fully launched in the world of television entertainment.

After the fifth season, Yvette left *A Different World* for a stint as a producer on ABC's *Hangin' with Mr. Cooper,* starring black stand-up comedian Mark Curry as a twenty-something teacher at an inner-city school. She felt she had something particularly unique to contribute because, again, she was the same age as the characters and could relate to them in a personal way.

The experience was less than gratifying, however, due to difficulties with staff members who believed it was better for women—especially black women—to be seen and not heard. As she told an online biographer, "They weren't used to people who looked like me being in the position of authority." Forced to deal with the reality that this was the norm in Hollywood, Yvette became determined to create her own environment.

Fortunately, the gods sometimes smile on those who actually deserve it, and opportunity arrived in the form of Kim Coles and Queen Latifah. Rap artist and actress Latifah and stand-up comedian Kim Coles had recently signed deals with the FOX network and Warner Brothers television to develop a series. But who would create it? Yvette Lee Bowser's (then Yvette Lee) name came up, and Warner Brothers executives approached her with an offer to create the show. She jumped at the chance.

> *Queen Latifah, Kim Coles, and Yvette shared a vision of* Living Single: *they wanted the show to speak the truth and do it with humor.*

Queen Latifah, Kim, and Yvette clicked immediately. The three shared a vision about what the show should reflect: not simply positive images of black women and men, but honest characterizations of people with whom they were all well acquainted. They wanted the show to speak the truth and do it with humor.

The result was *Living Single,* a series centered around six friends in New York trying to make sense of life and love in the '90s: Khadijah, the hard-driving publisher of *Flavor Magazine;* Max, a high-powered attorney; Synclaire, an innocent, free-spirited secretary; Regine, a self-proclaimed diva on a sugar-daddy hunt; Kyle, a stockbroker, buppie, and ladies' man; and Overton, ace philosopher and handyman.

The chemistry among the eclectic ensemble cast was potent, and the razor-edged humor attracted a strong audience across all demographic sectors. But the show found a permanent home in the hearts of black viewers, where it reigned for its duration. *Living Single* broke new ground in featuring strong female lead characters and won two NAACP Image awards for outstanding comedy.

Yvette's brilliant brainchild was so popular among audiences that when the show was slated for cancellation after four seasons, viewers organized a letter-writing campaign to save it. FOX relented and was forced to bring *Living Single* back for a new season. After the hoopla died down, however, FOX quietly canceled *Living Single* in the middle of the 1996–97 season. They did it without a lot of fanfare, so there was no advance notice to marshal forces for another protest.

Art Mirrors Life

YVETTE Lee Bowser sees an uncanny parallel between her professional path and her private life. When she began working as a writer's apprentice for the college-based show *A Different World,* she was a recent graduate of dorm life, bad food, class deadlines, and college romances found and lost. In her twenties, she created and produced *Living Single,* about twenty-something roommates and friends dealing with adult-life questions in all their variations. On the heels of *Living Single* came the short-lived, half-hour series *Lush Life,* which, like the Duke Ellington/Billy Strayhorn composition, was more visual jazz innovation than sitcom and possibly ahead of its time with its racially diverse cast and themes. *Lush Life* boasted a mixed-race lead character whose mother was white, mirroring Yvette's background.

So when Yvette married producer Kyle Bowser in 1994, it was easy to surmise that she was likely already composing in her head stories and dialogue for her latest creation, *For Your Love,* a comedy about the complexities of love and marriage. The show debuted on NBC in 1997 and did well in the ratings, building as it did on a lead-in from the hit show *Mad About You.* Even though *For Your Love* held the large audience *Mad About You* attracted, NBC dropped the show after only eight episodes, according to Yvette, because Warner Brothers would not relinquish its ownership. That meant that it would cost too much for NBC to continue to air the series.

> *Producers and studios are often locked into the mistaken mindset that black shows must adopt a specific tone to appeal to black audiences.*

The lack of black programming on television has garnered the networks a good deal of criticism from African Americans, Latinos, and other groups who are summarily underrepresented. At a recent Hollywood Radio and Television Society panel discussion about the portrayal and lack of minorities in the media, UPN Entertainment President Tom Nunan maintained that advertisers are part of the problem. There is a "tremendous amount" of pressure to segregate programming because the advertising community wants it that way, he said. According to Nunan, rather than mix programs that attract integrated audiences, advertisers want blocks of time dedicated to "specific demographic" groups.

Yvette disagrees with this analysis. "NBC chose ownership of certain shows over diversity," she says, adding that *For Your Love* kept the largely white viewership tuned in, evidence that there is no need to "segregate" programming to attract certain audiences. The problem, she states, is that producers and studios are often locked into the mistaken mindset that black shows must adopt a specific tone to appeal to black audiences and that "authentically" black programs will not translate for white audiences. "The advertisers are not the problem. It's the kind of programs that producers are creating," she observes. "When I tried to create something sophisticated, they said it wasn't 'black enough,' but every show that features us doesn't have to sound a certain way."

For Your Love has since moved to the more ethnically friendly WB. Starring Holly Robinson Peete and Deedee Pfeiffer (Michelle's little sister) among an impressive ensemble cast, *For Your Love* is now in its fourth season. Yvette's current focus is to take it to the next creative level: write strong stories, further develop the characters, tell the truth through their voices, and, in the process, make us laugh.

The Secret of Her Success

"THE secret of my success," says Yvette earnestly, "is that I've been creative but extremely honest in my storytelling." Her stories do tend to reflect a certain expansiveness, to reach beyond artificial barriers such as race and sex to explore topics and issues that resonate across the board. Her characters have probed everything from the foibles of everyday life to the controversial—date rape, gay acceptance, racism—to the never before broached—black-on-black prejudice. Yvette works easily with a diverse writing staff in an atmosphere that encourages the contribution of different perspectives to give the characters fuller lives and make them more like real people.

The tendency to encourage diversity in thinking and approach is a natural outgrowth of Yvette's life experience. Born in Philadelphia to a white mother and a black father who divorced when she was very young, Yvette grew up in California in a family without much money. Her mother had remarried, this time to a Japanese man, and they lived in various areas of Los Angeles before settling in racially diverse but rigidly segregated Santa Monica.

Yvette became adept at negotiating relationships with all sorts of people. As her mother's only child, she also developed (as only children often do) a healthy talent for introspection as well as the skills of an expert observer. All of this led to an ability to understand the motivations and desires of other people and a similarly insightful understanding of herself, both key to a writer's development. "Between the ages of five and twelve, I must have lived in eight different places," muses Yvette. "You don't have to live every experience to relate to it, but it made me creative."

She alludes to being both an insider and an outsider, a participant and a watcher, understandable given her journey from poor beginnings to wealth. Her personal struggle to overcome many obstacles, from being overweight to intraracial prejudice, has served to build in her an independently sustained sense of self and a deep empathy for others who weather their own personal storms. She can still feel the pain of being teased by her black half-brothers because she is half-white. She recalls vividly what it was like to live without the financial benefits that her young son, Evan, now two, can almost certainly take for granted.

> "*The secret of my success is that I've been creative but extremely honest in my storytelling.*"

Yvette recalls her mother proudly purchasing their first car, a pink DeSoto station wagon, when Yvette was in elementary school. While her mother had accomplished quite a feat in their straitened circumstances, Yvette was embarrassed. "It looked like a pink hippopotamus. It drew a lot of unwanted attention, and kids can really be cruel," says Yvette, wincing at the pain of the memory. Such experiences breathe poignant life as well as a little bit of Yvette into each of her characters. "The part of me that was ashamed definitely gave life to Regine [in *Living Single*]."

Yvette views these early experiences as having shaped her, rather than limited her. A self-described type-A personality, she always worked hard and set her sights high. "Coming from meager beginnings doesn't mean that I can't do whatever I want," she says. That message is the legacy she hopes to leave to those who may want to follow in her formidable footsteps.

"There's a lack of awareness that writing for television is an option for women and people of color," she says. "As African Americans, we don't have enough role models, we don't have people we can look at and say I want to be like that, a television writer. All we know is doctor, lawyer, engineer."

> *"As African Americans, we don't have enough role models, we don't have people we can look at and say I want to be like that, a television writer."*

Opening the Door for Others

YVETTE acknowledges that television is extremely competitive, it is hard to break through as a writer, and certain industry biases limit opportunities. It is generally difficult for black writers to get hired to write for "white" shows. And while it is easier for black writers to find a place on ethnic shows, those shows suffer the highest cancellation rates. Only about 18 of the 165 shows on network television feature blacks, and a fair share of those are on UPN. "Being black is not necessarily in vogue in Hollywood right now," says Yvette, echoing similar sentiments voiced by other writers and directors. "How many shows do you see that focus on black central characters? And when we are featured, *how* are we featured?"

With her commitment to diversity and fair representation on the screen, Yvette dedicates time and effort to discovering different voices to work for her behind the scenes. She mentors writers where and when she can because she believes it is absolutely necessary. As one of the few African American powers in Hollywood, she is uniquely positioned to teach and groom other women and people of color and is especially sensitive to what they may be feeling as people often seen as outsiders. She knows how important that kind of guidance is because she never really had it herself, and she sure could have used it.

In the best sense of the philosophy "each one, teach one," she hires women and people of color whenever an opportunity presents itself and makes a special effort to help black women writers. She is an exacting boss who works sixty hours a week and expects as much from her writers and staff as she does from herself—that type-A personality in action. "I can open doors," she says. "But it's up to the person to walk through. You've got to bring something to the party."

Her beneficent leanings are also in evidence outside the studio. Yvette lends her support to the NAACP, Alpha Kappa Alpha sorority, and the Los Angeles Mission. She is particularly proud to have sponsored the participation of fifteen inner-city children in the All God's Children Performing Arts Conservatory, which is devoted to opening the eyes and minds of young people to their own potential and the possibilities the world offers.

> "*How many shows do you see that focus on black central characters? And when we are featured,* how *are we featured?*"

For Yvette, love of what she does—whether it's supporting a good cause or producing a television show—is her motivating force. When you love your work, grueling as it may be, you usually do it well, she says, and success is a by-product of that.

Although her work love has been television, SisterLee Productions is branching out into feature films. "I really enjoy television because I like living with the same characters, but there's something intriguing about doing one well-told story," says Yvette. A one-hour comedy-drama, *The Miseducation of Piper Fein,* is already in development. Based loosely on Yvette's life, it tells the story of a young biracial woman in her early thirties who is trying to unravel the complexities of her life by reviewing the frivolity and dysfunction of her adolescent years. Yvette describes the project as *"The Blunder Years* meets *Love and Happiness."*

As a final piece of advice for those who might want to pursue a career in television, this comedy writer who turned funny into gold drops a pearl of perfect wisdom: "You can't take this too seriously."

2

Keeping Hope Alive

John Bryant

Chairman and CEO

Operation HOPE and Bryant Group Companies, Inc.

Los Angeles, California

Operation HOPE founded: 1992

Number of Employees: 33

Initial Investment: $5,000

HOPE Loans and Commitments: $81 million

JOHN BRYANT SAYS he will not run for national public office any time soon. That is America's loss. Cited for outstanding community and business achievements by presidents Ronald Reagan, George Bush, and Bill Clinton, *TIME* magazine, *Black Enterprise* magazine, and a host of other esteemed luminaries and publications, John arguably is the one person most responsible for rebuilding the war-torn communities of South Central Los Angeles that were virtually destroyed during riots in 1992.

As the founder of Operation HOPE, a nonprofit investment banking consortium, John is the catalyst for an infusion of home and business capital to revitalize a section of urban Los Angeles that had long been targeted by local, state, and federal officials for more economic investment, but until he stepped onto the scene was largely ignored.

Looking Back

A product of Compton, John had left the mean streets of South Central behind in both body and spirit years before. Without a college degree but plenty of heart and the fierce compulsion to excel, he got out as soon as he could. After much struggle and perhaps more than his share of failures, he finally found his niche as an investment broker, eventually founding Bryant Group Companies, Inc., a privately held enterprise involved in investment banking and several other business partnerships. The poor boy who formerly attended school in homemade suits was now a rich man, and he looked back on the people in his old community as lazy, shiftless, and unambitious. He believed that poor people were poor because that's what they deserved.

Then a nearly all-white jury acquitted four white Los Angeles policemen of all charges in their racially motivated, brutal beating of black motorist Rodney King, despite the fact that the beating was recorded on video by a resident in the area. Enraged people of color took to the streets of South Central Los Angeles, burning and looting in an uncontrolled frenzy of violence in reaction to the blatant injustice of a decision that confirmed what they already knew: justice for black people is a crapshoot with loaded dice, even when evidence of the crime is seemingly undeniable.

John Bryant was stunned by the verdict. He remembered thinking when he first heard about the case, "These officers are going down. This is America. It doesn't matter about the color of the jury." The verdict provided a moment of clarity, an epiphany so profound that he was moved to tears. "Here I was, a black man who had left his community and become successful, thinking discrimination didn't exist," said John in an interview a few years ago. "Let me tell you, watching the buildings burn the night after the verdict, part of me was on the streets rioting too. I wanted to—I had to—do something."

> *"Here I was, a black man who had left his community and become successful, thinking discrimination didn't exist."*

That night John realized that justice is often reserved, like preferred seating in an expensive restaurant, for the privileged few. Back in the working-class, working-poor, and just plain poor confines of South Central there is little justice. There is instead, as he remarks, just us.

The night the decision was announced, John closed his downtown offices and went to the First African Methodist Episcopal Church in the West Adams section of Los Angeles. The church became a meeting headquarters of sorts, where black community leaders and parishioners gathered to pray, debate, and strategize about what to do post-verdict and in light of the violence that had overtaken the city. Along with hundreds of others, John went to the church every day for three days, trapped in a fog of disillusionment over the unfairness of the system and at a loss as to what he could do to help rebuild the community and his faith in the system. Finally, the Reverend Cecil Murray said to him, "You're a banker; put your talents to work."

Shaken out of his shell-shocked immobility, John took $5,000 of his own money and founded Operation HOPE, his "guilt-ridden" answer to the destruction in the wake of civil unrest that he believes was as much in reaction to economic disparity, hopelessness, and despair as it was to the Rodney King verdict. "There is a difference between being broke and being poor," says John. "Broke means you don't have any money; poor is a frame of mind."

> *"As James Brown said, 'Open up the door and I'll get it myself.' Black people have always been bootstrappers. We just don't always start from the same place."*

John was determined to help break that mind lock under the theory that economic investment in inner-city communities, a first step toward economic equality, will result in the return of those areas and a domino-effect reduction in crime, poverty, and social breakdown. "You don't burn that which you own," he explains. At the same time, he believed that investment in South Central could be profitable and that it should be viewed in terms of its possibilities, a win-win situation for investors and beneficiaries. This was important because John Bryant knows that black folks don't want or need a handout, but a hand up. "You know what James Brown said: 'Open up the door and I'll get it myself.' We [black people] have always been bootstrappers. We just don't always start off from the same place," says John.

Bankers on the Bus

JOHN swung into action. He called bankers he had brokered money-making deals for in the past, put them on a chartered bus, and drove them through the burned-out rubble and quiet tree-lined streets so that they could see the opportunities John envisioned. He persuaded his colleagues that they could "do well by doing good" and that loans in these areas made good economic sense. The people of South Central, argued John, were underserved. Here was a chance not just to create jobs and services, but to create a market. The pockets of South Central where the working class lived had been long overlooked and there was money to be made. And even though they might have less than outstanding credit, they had other assets, according to John. "They had been paying rent and utility bills and making car payments faithfully," he said, and that should count for something.

Moreover, John pointed out, African Americans represent the ninth largest consumer buying power in the world, which translates into more than $21 billion annually in California alone. In addition, he said, not a single home was burned during the riots, lending weight to his assertion that people don't destroy what they hold a stake in. Banks had additional incentive to participate. The federally monitored Community Reinvestment Act requires that banks find ways to loan money to low-income but creditworthy communities. Doing well by doing good started to make a lot of sense to those bankers on the bus.

Since 1992, Operation HOPE has brokered $36 million in loans, with another $45 million in commitments to the program. The fifty banks that are part of the Operation HOPE alliance represent $1.7

> *African Americans represent the ninth largest consumer buying power in the world, which translates into more than $21 billion annually in California alone.*

trillion in combined assets. No bank has ever pulled out of the consortium and only four of the over three hundred homeowners who have received loans have defaulted on them. In addition, Operation HOPE has educated over 10,000 adults about loans, investments, credit, and personal finances in general. It has set up a training program in economic literacy for young people, to prepare the next generation to become stakeholders in the community.

At thirty-three, John Bryant has succeeded in his goal to build a bridge between two worlds that rarely meet. Acting as the diplomatic envoy employed to bring both to the table, John serves as the interpreter and translator between them, patiently breaking down stereotypes and facilitating some measure of understanding one small step at a time. It is appropriate work for a man who says his vision is, simply, to change the world.

In the Beginning

JOHN Bryant started his first business at the age of ten as a wholesale candy seller specializing in the brands of candy kids in his Compton neighborhood wanted to buy. Capitalized by his mother with an investment of $40, he learned how to buy candy wholesale from the guy who owned the liquor store. In those days, the liquor store doubled as the neighborhood candy stop on the way to school. Little did the liquor store owner know that he was training the competition. After his impromptu lesson on the art of buying, John went down to Iris Food Store and bought the candy he knew his friends would want, and then set about picking a location for the venture. All the kids looking for that morning sweet-tooth fix were perpetually late for school because the liquor store was out of the way. So, John found a place conveniently on the way to school and "created a niche market." At the pinnacle of his career as a candy-selling tycoon, he made $300 a week.

> *John Bryant started his first business at the age of ten. At the pinnacle of this career as a candy-selling tycoon, he made $300 a week.*

It seems that from the beginning, John Bryant was destined for highs and lows, with very little that could pass for in-between. When he was ten, his mother, a sewing-machine operator at Boeing Aircraft for thirty-three years, dressed him in custom-made Little Lord Fauntleroy purple velour suits. He speculates it was because she wanted him to stand apart from the crowd. He credits this effort to make him stick out like a sore thumb as partially responsible for his success today. His perpetual motion forward ("while you're sleeping, I'm working") is a result of striving for the respect he never got as a kid. "She wanted me to become an individual," says John. As a consequence of all the merciless teasing, he set his sights high and worked harder.

His parents divorced when he was young and, at the age of thirteen, John moved in with his father, a concrete contractor in Compton. His dad put him to work for the business. Neither parent had finished high school,

> *John credits his mother's effort to make him stick out like a sore thumb as partially responsible for his success today.*

so they encouraged him to get an education. John was ahead of the curve and had a plan. He convinced his father to send him to the Hollywood Professional School, a private institution that catered to kids in "the business." The best part of it for John was the discovery that school ended at lunchtime so that students could go to the film set.

Environment has a way of encouraging participation and, in a relatively short period of time, John fell into acting. Not very good at it even by his own estimation, he nevertheless landed parts, including bit roles on the '70s sitcom *Diff'rent Strokes*. At the height, he was making thousands a week, which was both a blessing and a curse. John became a kid-star cliché, blowing his money on a house in Malibu, cars, and women. He also acquired an arrogance to match his income, although both would be short lived. By the time he was seventeen, his acting career was a memory. His lack of real acting ability caught up with him and the parts stopped coming.

Unable to get acting jobs, he took a job as a waiter at an upscale restaurant in Malibu, where his combustible combination of charm, wit, and intelligence caught the eye of an investment banker named Harvey Baskin, who took a liking to the brash but talented young man.

Baskin took him out of the restaurant and put him to work in corporate America, mentoring him in the art of deal making. John did not apply those lessons well in the beginning. "When I left acting, I looked for some way to leverage my funds," says John. "But I led with my ego and began believing my own press. Then I started making bad business decisions."

That might be an understatement. For some unfathomable reason, John created a concert production company, and his first project centered around revitalizing the career of the lead singers of the Platters, a defunct doo-wop group whose popularity had ended by the time John was born. Stubbornly refusing to heed better judgment, he poured money into the venture, renting a concert center out in the middle of nowhere, hiring limousines, and spending a small fortune on promotional materials. It was a disaster of epic proportions. He lost six figures and ended up sleeping in his Jeep for six months. "That's where I learned you give the market what it wants, not what you want," says John.

Undeterred, he hatched a scheme to import FILA sportswear and slashed prices to undercut other sellers, a venture that resulted in a threat of a suit for unfair business practices. A lecture series on how to start a business also fizzled, as did other nonstarters, too many to name, he says.

Then, John was referred to a man named Stephen Cotter, an investment banker and the chairman of Wade, Cotter and Company, a specialty investment organization. Harking back to what he had learned from Harvey Baskin, John managed to be hired by the firm, despite some reservations on the company's part. "This was definitely an affirmative action gig," recalls John. "I was a charity case."

Wade, Cotter and Company started him in the field of equity lending, which John describes more colorfully as making loans to black people who can't afford to pay the money back so the loan company ends up owning the house. It was there that he began to understand what he terms "unconscious racism" or, perhaps more accurately, involuntary racism. The company took advantage of folks who were vulnerable and those folks were black.

"They could charge ten to twelve percent interest, but these guys just wanted a high return on their money." They weren't out to hurt black people per se but they were willing to exploit them. John, recognizing that he would be hurting his own community, could not in good conscience do the same.

The situation started him thinking that it was possible to get the same return legitimately by making loans to individuals who were actually able to pay the installments. John knew, whether or not Wade, Cotter and Company was aware of it, that those people actually do exist. Not only do they exist but, in Central Los Angeles, the default rate is about half that of more affluent white neighborhoods. There are black people with money, he told his bosses, people who pay their bills on time. These thoughts gave rise to a full-blown John Bryant brainstorm.

> *The loan default rate in Central Los Angeles is about half that of more affluent white neighborhoods.*

Outrunning Failure

JOHN pitched Wade, Cotter and Company on the notion of creating a whole new division that would make short-term loans to folks with bad credit but enough assets to collateralize default should it come to that. In his characteristic all-or-nothing way, he promised to work for free, asking only that Wade lend the company its name and its Rolodex. John promised them half of the profits.

In 1990, Wade reluctantly spawned WCC Funding Corporation. "I was one employee and I had an office," says John. "I failed the real estate exam a third time and I did no business in the first year." Wade,

Cotter had little to lose, so they hung in there for another year and John, consummate salesman that he is, brought in $9 million in year two. He accomplished this feat by working his network; his first client was referred to him by a friend and it just grew from there. "I just outran failure," he laughs, adding that success is actually just the ability to keep going in spite of what has happened, to keep pushing until things change for the better. "No matter how bad my luck was, I could make my own luck. Hank Aaron had the most home runs of all time, but he had the most strikeouts too."

WCC provided financing for whichever good bet walked in the door, no matter how odd, including an heiress to the Forbes fortune who needed a quick, short-term loan, which she guaranteed with her alimony payments.

The third year, John racked up $15 million in sales, and in the fourth year, $24 million. By this time, Wade, Cotter was having its own problems. John bought out the division and started his own company, which operates now under the umbrella of Bryant Group Companies, Inc.

The relationships he established during his tenure with WCC stood him in good stead when he founded Operation HOPE in 1992. "I was never really a banker," says John. "I was a deal maker. All the deals I did were with small community banks and they were good deals, so when the riots came around the bankers were willing to do the bus tour. They trusted me."

Indeed. Although the city's riot recovery organization, Rebuild L.A., became mired in politics and more or less ground to a halt under the weight of the egos on the board as well as a lack of trust (banks were nervous about putting money into commercial ventures in areas where, when residents got mad, they burned down businesses), the mortgage-lending side of the equation has been an unequivocal success.

John started Operation HOPE, he says, because he believes the people living there need help to jump-start a trend of revitalization that benefits all the players, not donations, not welfare. "Charity," he insists, "is condescending. In 1999, it's about empathy, not sympathy."

And he has convinced other capitalists—which is the camp in which he squarely places himself—that it is possible to help people and make money at the same time. Moreover, he has persuasively argued that the world is becoming a much smaller place and that cutting off certain communities means limiting the marketplace, that a failure to invest in human capital is a costly mistake on several levels. John insists that it is impossible to outrun the problems in urban areas by moving out of the city. Carjackings, crime, and other problems are beginning to commute to the suburbs. The only way to sleep soundly at night is to address the issues now.

> *John insists that it is impossible to outrun the problems in urban areas by moving out of the city. The only way to sleep soundly at night is to address the issues now.*

"Not to reinvest in people," John says, "is cannibalizing your community." He says it simply, as if it is a fact everyone should simply know, just as they should understand that he is not arguing for social equality or civil rights. Not that he doesn't support the idea; it's just not what he does. "What I care about is that [banks] put resources on the table to leverage. I don't come at people with emotion because business is not personal and the stats will tell you—white, black, or yellow, it's about green."

The Man Behind HOPE

EVEN given his tremendous success, John would not necessarily advise people to follow his particularly rough and pitted path to the top, and he hopes that the next generation will aspire to reach higher than he did, anyway. "My model is not the ideal model for most people," he says. "Folks should load up in degrees and walk in the door so that they cannot be denied a seat at the table."

One wall of John's office is covered with citations, awards, and pictures, a display that some have criticized as a show of ego. He heatedly disputes that. "I have a credentials wall in my office so that I cannot be denied on merit. My accomplishments are indisputable and the question is answered even before it has been asked."

Hubris, ego, and arrogance are recurring themes in the story of John Bryant, words that he either uses to describe himself or that others toss out with regularity. It is true that he is self-assured, assertive, handsome, and a mesmerizing presence. Complex, yes. Egotistical, no. Operation HOPE requires too much of a commitment, too much grunt work for a dedicated narcissist. On his home answering machine, John once had a recorded message that sums him up pretty well. It said:

> *Welcome to the world of one of America's optimists, where perception is stronger than fact, where honesty is reality and dreams come true.*

Welcome to the world of one of America's optimists, John Bryant, where perception is stronger than fact, where honesty is reality and dreams come true. Where self-love, self-esteem, and self-worth can be easily misunderstood. Within that world, those who dwell in the past rob the future. And those who neglect the past steal from the present. It is obvious that you are either special or important, or chances are you wouldn't have this number. So please leave your message and remember: Never do anything you cannot live with, or walk away from anyone that you cannot live without.

Clearly, John has a potent charm that people find compelling, the kind of charisma that cannot be bought or taught. Any politician would kill for his ability to inspire trust and respect. If he could bottle it, he'd be even richer. But although John is wealthy, money is not the be-all, end-all. It is not what makes John Bryant tick.

No one knows that better than Elizabeth Booker, his girlfriend and best friend, who is a senior vice president at Wells Fargo in Texas and a power in her own right. The woman he affectionately calls Effie sees a side of John that most folks are not privileged to view. "He has a strong ego," she concedes, "but he always checks the pulse of the people around him. And he listens. Some people, you're just talking at them, but he listens."

In addition to being a capitalist with a heart, away from the spot-light John is a philanthropist. Effie reports that last Christmas he went into the kitchen of a restaurant he frequents to wish the staff a happy holiday and to give them gifts for their children. He did it qui-etly, with no fanfare, simply for the joy of giving.

John and Effie are also both intensely spiritual people. John reads a lot about spiritual healing, his way of keeping himself replenished, according to Effie, who speaks for them both when she says they don't operate without God in their life. Of his reaction to the L.A. riots, she says it was not just an effort to assuage his guilt about leaving a community behind. He agrees and says that Operation HOPE was also his personal mission, his attempt to make himself "transparent to God's will."

Now, John is giving thanks. "My life has been blessed," he says. Indeed, he has much to be grateful for, as do the people of South Central Los Angeles and the banks that have learned to do well by doing good. Over a few short years and almost single-handedly, John Bryant has accomplished the kind of urban economic investment, re-development, and revitalization that Washington policy wonks and politicians have been theorizing about, promising, and talking to death since widespread, hard-core urban blight started to creep up on cities twenty-five years ago.

If John ever does decide to run for national office, it ought to be a cakewalk. But for now, America's loss is one city's gain.

3

For Us, By Us

J. Alexander Martin, Vice President and Head Designer

Daymond John, President and CEO

Carl Brown, Co-founder

Keith Perrin, Co-founder

FUBU

New York, New York

Founded: 1992

1998 Revenues: $350 million

Number of Employees: 85

Initial Investment: $105,000

THEY ARE HIP-HOP and Wall Street. Straight out of the 'hood and Fortune 500 bound, they have combined their knowledge of street style with an entrepreneurial instinct and skills equal to those of any Wharton or Harvard Business School grad. The result is a casual clothing business that has big competitors looking over their shoulders and consumers flocking to buy.

The founders of the FUBU ("for us, by us") sportswear company—president and CEO Daymond John and partners J. Alexander Martin, Carl Brown, and Keith Perrin—never dreamed that what began in 1992 as a home factory producing tie-top hats would eventually become a $350 million clothing business.

FUBU's 1998 earnings ($350 million) catapulted it out of the bush leagues and into contention with such labels as Donna Karan ($670 million) and Tommy Hilfiger ($847 million). Unlike these clothing giants, which also court the young African American urban market, FUBU speaks an original dialect of the fashion language, one with a richer, more expressive intonation. Oversize sweatshirts, leather jackets, baggy jeans, t-shirts, hats—all boast original and bold color combinations, sophisticated styling, and a distinctive logo. These high-quality clothes have come to define hip-hop chic. The men's line, FUBU The Collection, is carried in more than 5,000 stores nationwide—including Macy's, Nordstrom, and FootLocker—and the women's line is available in over 5,000 specialty and department stores in the United States and abroad. FUBU expects to open its first free-standing store in Manhattan by the end of 1999.

For Us, By Us

"FOR us, by us" is more about attitude and pace-setting, cutting-edge style than it is about racial unity or exclusion, although black culture exerts a powerful influence on popular culture. From music to movies to the fashion runways of New York, black style and innovation drive what is hip and new. So it follows that since FUBU has appeal in the city, it has appeal in the suburbs. Like hip-hop music, FUBU is universal. Yet, it cannot be denied that race is part of what contributed to its genesis and to the success of the FUBU brand.

While businesses are happy to make money off black consumers, few businesses and products are willing to come across as "too black," a schizophrenic irony recently detailed in a *Wall Street Journal* article about black businesses that adopt any number of strategies to avoid appearing too ethnic, including hiring white front people to interact with customers.

> *FUBU's founders never dreamed that what began in 1992 as a home factory producing tie-top hats would eventually become a $350 million clothing business.*

Daymond John created FUBU partially in response to the fact that other clothiers run from the association with black consumers. "They said they didn't need to make their clothes for African Americans," remarks Daymond, so he decided to launch his own personal affirmative action movement.

FUBU sends a potent message about the power of black dollars and the need for more African Americans to become producers and not just consumers, to fill the void where there is an economic opportunity. The creation of black business bolsters the economic well-being of the African American community as much as it does the individual entrepreneurs because it generates black wealth and often jobs for African Americans. Wealth equals power. The four founders of FUBU recognized that truth and instinctively understood that economic empowerment and all it entails—freedom, control, and wealth—come from ownership.

From the Street

AT the base of FUBU's success is a clothing philosophy and style that take their cue from the street, from what's real. "We instinctively knew we were good salesmen. And we knew that promotion, market-ing, and distribution were important," says Carl Brown, whose job is to oversee a bit of everything in the company. But when it comes down to it, "we design what we want to wear. That's our vibe."

A close connection to real people is part of what makes FUBU unique. While other designers employ "style scouts" to go out and re-port back about what's new on the street, the FUBU guys already know because that's where they come from. As Daymond John says:

> *FUBU sends a potent message about the power of black dollars and the need for more African Americans to become producers and not just consumers.*

"I don't read *GQ* to follow fash-ion. I go to parties, restaurants, the car wash." The fluid give-and-take between FUBU and its wearers is serious. The company is likely to receive upwards of five thousand e-mails a day, containing feedback, questions, and often detailed design ideas. And the FUBU men pay atten-tion to their public.

But, while the owners are readily hailed for their mastery at marketing "urban" or "street" fashions to young African American men, the praise from others in the fashion world and the mainstream and business press generally typically stops there. They are rarely lauded for their business acumen, which is clearly demonstrated by FUBU's phenomenal rise under the founders' careful management. Further proof lies in the fact that the company is now worth over a third of a billion dollars and the originators are still largely in control of the corporation.

What started as hats sold on the street expanded to include every-thing from women's fashions to tailored suits, leather ankle boots, and accessories. The partners oversaw expansion of the business while re-taining their own integrity and that of the product. This is no small feat because in the image-conscious fashion industry (as in many businesses) perception is everything and the temptation to shut up and go along is strong.

For example, when some store buyers suggested removing the FUBU "hang tag," the designer identifier attached to each article of clothing that pictures the native-Queens quartet in t-shirts, baggy jeans, and caps turned backward, the men adamantly refused. However they are perceived, FUBU's founders will not compromise their dignity for someone else's comfort or their own profit, an admirable rarity in a world where the almighty dollar regularly buys souls wholesale. Now, of course, those same stores are clamoring for FUBU because it is a hot commodity among young blacks *and* whites, as evidenced by the fact that Washington State, a predominantly white area of the country, is one of their largest markets.

The four partners are the quintessential opposite of what we are conditioned to believe the owners of a multimillion-dollar corporation should look like. They are incredibly young (in their late twenties and early thirties), on the quiet side, serious (a fun-loving playfulness lurks underneath), just regular guys. Instead of "Nice to meet you," it's "Wassup?" The kick is that the guys in the white button-down shirts and ties running around their office work for *them*.

It is clear that the partners are dead serious about business, while at the same time keeping their success in perspective: they are completely at peace with the notion that it could all be gone tomorrow. The FUBU team built a recognizable and highly desirable brand out of nothing. Literally. But it is no happy accident that FUBU is what it is today. FUBU is not a fluke, it is not about serendipity, it is not simply about luck. It is about sweat, grit, endurance, and resilience.

What the FUBU team didn't know they sought to learn by experience, observation, reasoning, or the process of elimination. The untold story about FUBU is that four young African American men in their twenties decided to take charge of their destinies and carve a place in the business world for themselves on their own terms. They are the embodiment of Booker T. Washington's famous saying: "A man must be self-made before he is ever made."

The Journey

IN 1992, the childhood friends were doing what they could to keep body and soul together. Daymond John was waiting tables at Red Lobster and running a commuter van service. J. Martin had been a member of the military, and Keith Perrin and Carl Brown worked a succession of jobs—real estate management, loading trucks, whatever paid the rent. Daymond and his partners never went to college. The four are matter-of-fact about it. It was all they could do to survive in working-class Queens; higher education was an out-of-reach luxury. Keith says it simply: "My mom was poor. We couldn't afford to pay for college."

That didn't stop them from seeking other routes to success and keeping an eye out for opportunity. So when Daymond became frustrated by his inability to find a tie-top hat (a close-fitting knit hat that ties on top) he liked, as legend has it, Carl suggested he buy some material to make his own. If Daymond had trouble finding hats he liked, didn't it stand to reason that other brothers out there might be having the same problem? He made some hats to sell and wound up selling forty in a day, earning, to his surprise, $800. Daymond concluded that opportunity had just walked up and tapped him on the shoulder.

The untold story about FUBU is that four young African American men in their twenties decided to take charge of their destinies.

Daymond conceived the name "for us, by us," added the distinctive acronym to the hats (and later to everything else), and invited his boys J., Carl, and Keith, to join him in the venture. The only one who had an intrinsic love of the clothing business was J., who had been a student at the Fashion Institute of Technology in New York. (He is the authority on color and takes the lead on FUBU design, although three of the four partners must agree before any design is green-lighted.) The others were more attracted by the idea of starting and running their own business, as a way to make a living and "control their own destinies."

They knew it would not be easy. The four kept their day jobs and worked literally around the clock. As Carl puts it, "We had no life." Daymond did all the sewing, while the others did the cutting, packing, distribution, and selling. They made between twenty and forty hats a night to sell on the streets of Queens and to place in mom-and-pop stores on consignment. The team credits J. with keeping them motivated and focused when the schedule got to them or morale was low. He, they say, always had the ability to envision the future and "take it to the next level."

> *Any good marketing or public relations strategy relies heavily on perception. The partners promoted the perception that FUBU was both ubiquitous and hot.*

In the beginning, customers didn't find FUBU; FUBU found the customers. And they courted the market while they built a reputation. For four years, they put all of the money they made back into the business, taking no income from the company. By 1993, FUBU was gaining popularity on the street and the partners decided it was time to move to the next stage, which meant finding a way to gain wider attention and recognition for the brand. They hit on the idea of strategic product placement, preferably in a music video. Music videos are a perfect outlet—free celebrity advertising, frequently repeated during the televised play cycle. Performers have a huge impact on fashion trends, and videos directly target the young style-conscious consumer.

Any good marketing or public relations strategy relies heavily on perception, and it was the intention of the partners to promote the perception that FUBU was both ubiquitous and hot: even if everybody isn't wearing it, make it look like everybody who's anybody is.

Business On the Rise

THE FUBU team decided to pursue superstar rapper and actor LL Cool J as their celebrity spokesmodel. They had an advantage in that they had all grown up in the same Queens neighborhood and Daymond had known LL since his teens. But nothing in business comes easy and LL Cool J didn't either. Daymond approached him repeatedly with the request to wear FUBU. He didn't say yes and the partners didn't take no for an answer. Finally, Daymond started camping out on the video set and in front of LL Cool J's house in Queens.

Whether it was persistence or the clothes, LL finally agreed to pose in a FUBU t-shirt for a promotional photograph. The photograph later appeared in the hip-hop magazine *The Source,* and a relationship was born. Now, LL Cool J is the primary FUBU spokesman, but the brand's chic has seduced other stars as well, including Mariah Carey, Janet Jackson, Will Smith, Whitney Houston, Busta Rhymes, and Sean (Puffy) Combs. FUBU products often appear on television shows, including *The Wayans Brothers, Sister, Sister, The Parent 'Hood,* and *Clueless.* And as an indication of the ageless appeal of FUBU, it should be noted that Patti LaBelle and Isaac Hayes are also FUBU loyalists.

The stamp of approval from the entertainment world has been crucial, according to Daymond. "A lot of the consumers can relate to the primaries of the company [the four partners]," he says. "But we're also different because the artists support us."

But in 1993, FUBU was just another face in the crowd, albeit an interesting face and one that was gaining recognition. After the LL Cool J photo, the FUBU partners started giving interviews, and other rap groups, such as Brand Nubian, got hip to the line. FUBU branched out to showing their designs at trade shows such as Black Expo, an annual convention where black businesses showcase their products. Black Expo provided important contacts, not only with possible commercial distribution outlets, but with consumers as well. At one show, the partners remember, a young woman arrived in a cut-off FUBU t-shirt, which started people clamoring for the style. Feedback like that is money in the bank.

On their way to breaking the surface, the team took to the road again for more trade shows, including the 1994 Magic Expo in Las Vegas, an annual gathering where the hottest, name-making fashion trends are shown. Although FUBU could not afford to rent a booth at the convention, they could afford to rent a hotel room. One hotel room. About five miles outside Vegas city limits. Undaunted, they mailed out postcards inviting store buyers to view the latest FUBU fashions in their hotel room. To their surprise, buyers from some of the most cutting-edge stores took them up on the invitation, including Dr. Jay's in New York and The Lark in Chicago, both of which sell to the up-to-the-minute, style-slave young and have the power to greatly influence the cachet of a brand. FUBU took in orders for $300,000 in clothes. They needed work space and capital. Quick.

Hurdling Obstacles

DAYMOND John did what any enterprising young man would do: he made the rounds to banks, twenty or thirty of them. But, as he told *Entrepreneur Magazine,* "[N]o one would give us a contract or a small business loan. No one believed in us."

The partners relish the fact that, now, those same potential investors come and sit in the lobby of FUBU's suite of offices in the Empire State Building, with no appointment, seeking an audience with the brothers they dismissed without a second thought five years ago.

With nowhere else to turn, in 1994, Daymond mortgaged his house in Queens, the one thing of significant value he owned, the one thing he had to show for years of hard work. With $100,000 from the second mortgage and $5,000 J. had saved, they turned the bottom floor of Daymond's house into a factory. In a demonstration of their faith and commitment to the business, his partners moved into the house to save money. They slept in shifts and then worked again, almost around the clock.

The commitment was paying off. By 1995, FUBU annual sales had reached $1 million and investors came knocking. The FUBU men did not acquiesce to the first knock but from the outset scrutinized the offers closely, separating those that should be considered from those that warranted a "no, thank you." Having already put everything into a venture no one had believed in except them, FUBU wasn't about to cave in at the first hint of money, even though they needed the infusion of cash badly.

> *A hallmark of the FUBU partners' perspective on the business is their attitude that they started with nothing and nothing is guaranteed.*

"All kinds of shady characters and strong people came to FUBU," recalls J. Martin. "But they wanted too big a piece of the company. When you've worked this hard, you have to do your homework. Even though our back was against the wall, we weren't going to sell out for financing."

"We've always been the underdog," adds Carl. "We had nothing to lose." So they held back, weighing the offers, and finally negotiated a deal with the Korean-based Samsung company to capitalize and distribute the FUBU line.

Lessons Learned

A hallmark of the FUBU partners' perspective on the business is their attitude that they started with nothing and nothing is guaranteed. As a consequence, they have the courage to take more risks and no fear of returning to square one if, God forbid, they should lose it all and have to make it happen a second time. Unlike business people who lose sight of who they are, confusing their identities with money and power, the FUBU team is clear-headed, grounded, real. Their philosophy is that life will deal you setbacks, so expect it, be flexible, and be willing to do whatever needs to be done to accomplish your goal. "Even if you have to start over from the beginning, do it," says Keith, whose job is to oversee product placement, marketing, and promotion, among other duties.

The FUBU team is always on the lookout for what they may need to change or adjust to keep themselves and the business on track. Most people, they say, are unwilling to change their attitudes, how they view a problem or life. The FUBU guys try to maintain open minds, to remain teachable and able to see the moral of the story. That is an important attribute because, in the beginning, like most entrepreneurs, they learned everything through trial and error.

Take the purple "foamy" jacket. It was bad but, ultimately, just a lovely dream. The guys had purchased the special material and created the design. The jacket turned out to be far too costly to mass produce. They still have the foamy, purple material.

For the longest time, recalls Carl, "that material looked at us and we looked at it." They kept it as a reminder that it is vitally important to research an idea in its entirety before resources and time are committed to its realization.

What they have done right is to expand the FUBU name and product recognition through licensing agreements, including contracts with Jordache and the National Basketball Association. The partners understand that they must mature and grow with their consumers, so they are scheduled to introduce a line of tailored suits in 1999, in connection with upscale tailored-clothing maker Pietrafesa, based in Syracuse, New York. They are also considering a line of FUBU eyewear, fragrance, and watches.

Success Means More Hard Work

THE FUBU tale has elements of the Cinderella story, but the partners still work fifteen-hour days. With great success comes great responsibility. "Five o'clock is lunchtime," says Keith.

Part of their inspiration is the working-class enclave of Queens itself, which has produced its share of successful entrepreneurs, including FUBU role model Russell Simmons, the multimillionaire founder of Def Jam Records and also the owner of a fledgling clothing line. Queens is also the home of doctors, lawyers, and small business owners (including Carl Brown's entrepreneurial grandfather) who left an indelible impression on the FUBU partners. "We grew up around working-class people," said Keith. "So we knew if you worked hard, you could have your own."

> "*We grew up around working-class people. So we knew if you worked hard, you could have your own.*"

They also read. Early on, Daymond bought everybody in the company a copy of the book *Think and Grow Rich,* by Napoleon Hill. First published in 1937, Hill's book is the spiritual antecedent of such books as *The 7 Habits of Highly Effective People* and *The Millionaire Next Door.* Generally considered a classic of the genre, *Think and Grow Rich,* inspired by the life experience of self-made millionaire Andrew Carnegie, may be one of the most influential books ever written on personal achievement and financial independence. It had an enormous impact on Daymond.

The partners applied all the teachings of the book to the development and growth of FUBU. "You say you're going to take the lessons seriously and subliminally you do," Daymond says. They employed the lessons about self-reliance and delayed gratification and the practical instruction that good businesspeople offer superior quality for the price. While FUBU clothes are far from cheap (jackets can run between $500 and $800, ankle boots are $130, and underwear costs around $20), they are less expensive than similar items manufactured by Hilfiger, Karan, and Ralph Lauren. In addition, the quality of the fabric, workmanship, color, and design are close to luxurious, and the clothing is still about fifteen percent lower in cost than the competitors'. Says Daymond: "I put a lot of quality into what I sell."

FUBU has been castigated for its prices, which is curious given that similar clothing lines and other popular name brands—Nike, for instance—charge as much or more without taking any heat.

But criticism is inevitable and FUBU has received its share over the past couple of years, from the pricing complaints to those who believe the company's bottom line will suffer as more white kids buy the clothes and thus lessen the street-cool quotient. Some clothing business analysts who follow the impact of trends on profits and stability believe that companies like FUBU and other hip-hop labels, such as Phat Farm and Wu-Wear, only have the power to influence design and boost the business overall, but lack the lasting power of established houses like Hilfiger. Maybe. But the hip-hop lines seem to be gaining domestic market share while they prepare to enter the international market aggres-

It is important for young people to know that you can live as well as the guy on the corner selling drugs without resorting to that dangerous life.

sively. According to Russell Simmons, one-third of the customer base for his Phat Farm line is in Asia. That bodes well for FUBU and others seeking to expand their customer base.

Help Me Help You

THE four still live near Queens and try to give back to the community in traditional ways by speaking about their experiences and success at schools and churches. They have also established the FUBU Foundation, a charitable giving organization. But perhaps most important, they make themselves accessible and are around as an example for all those who need role models. They believe it is important for folks in the neighborhood, especially young people, to talk to them, touch them, and know that you can live as well as the guy on the corner selling drugs without resorting to the dangerous and often fatal life of hustling. The partners report that they are constantly approached by people old and young who are excited and inspired by their success. "When people walk up to us on the street, they can't believe we're cool," says Keith.

Where rap holds the symbolic key to a better life, FUBU leads by example. The partners get frequent calls from young people who want to start their own clothing lines, but their example also provides motivation for people in all spheres of life. J. tells of a woman from Texas who places low-income workers in jobs. She called the FUBU partners to tell them that they were the inspiration for her work.

People who just want a job now that FUBU has become incredibly profitable also frequently approach the FUBU founders. For them, the guys have a tough love message: Go to school and get an education. Nothing comes easy, they tell folks, and encourage those who think they can coast to wealth without sweat and hard work to think again.

"Make it easy for somebody to help," Carl says, referring to the need for anyone who wants success to prepare for it by first getting an education. "Help me help you." The FUBU founders were willing to make the venture a success, to quote Malcolm X, "by any means necessary." They exhort those who would follow in their footsteps to take that message to heart: The world is yours if you work hard enough for it, but nothing is free.

CHAPTER 4

Fly Guy

Robin Petgrave
President
Bravo Helicopter and Wing
Torrance, California

Founded: 1991
1998 Revenues: $2.9 million
Number of Employees: 50, plus 26 instructor pilots
Initial Investment: $300
Current Net Worth: $4 million

Robin petgrave started Bravo Helicopter and Wing with $300 and an attitude. The $300 wasn't much, but the attitude was a real driving force.

"I started this business out of spite," he declares. The story goes that Robin was working at a flight training school when one day his boss wanted him to fly a less than well maintained helicopter. When Robin refused to do it, the guy grounded him for four days. Robin took the little money he had and walked. Forty-eight hours later, he started his own flight school. That response fits with his personality: he is impulsive, free-spirited, and a bit eccentric. And he can fly the hell out of almost anything.

Based in the Los Angeles area, Robin built Bravo Helicopter and Wing into a $4 million business that offers not only flight training, but air tour, sightseeing, and limousine services, as well as aviation for Hollywood movie and television production. Bravo is now one of the largest flight schools in the world and the largest helicopter tour service in California, with fifty employees, twenty-six instructor pilots, and more than thirty aircraft.

> *Robin is impulsive, free-spirited, and a bit eccentric. And he can fly the hell out of almost anything.*

Although the company has taken wing since its 1991 inception, Bravo is probably just one stop along the line of what will be a full, varied, and interesting career life for Robin. After all, before he launched Bravo, Robin had already won praise as an actor and been a world-class runner who just missed placing in the 400-yard hurdle and attending the 1984 Olympics. Since he is good at any number of things, his name will likely crop up at some later date attached to a new venture, one of the myriad ideas he tosses off regularly. Robin thrives on challenge and is unconstrained by the iron-tight psychic bonds that stop most of us from leaving our nine-to-fives. His life philosophy is summed up not by "what if?" but by "why not?"

Perhaps the most striking thing about Robin—a man who is as likely to show up at work in a tuxedo as he is in a flight suit—is that he seems to inspire devotion, loyalty, and trust among those who work with him. The people in Bravo's office radiate satisfaction. They really love their work and Robin. The feeling is mutual. The fact that he and his staff have such high regard for each other makes Bravo's success just that much more gratifying for its owner.

An Idea Takes Flight

ROBIN Petgrave, thirty-seven, is a maverick with a love of adventure and a tendency to follow where his instincts lead, which he insists is less about confidence than stubbornness. It is true that when Robin has an idea—whether it is brilliant or seemingly moronic—he is likely to see it through. As a result, his story is not a textbook example of entrepreneurship, nor a step-by-step guide. The classic jokester (he bills himself informally as a "flyin' ho—if you pay us we go"), he also possesses the serious qualities that separate successful business runners from the pack. He is goal oriented, tenacious, self-assured, flexible, and forgiving—when he stumbles, which he admits happens often, he deals with it and moves on. But Robin is unlikely to make the same mistake twice.

In 1991, Robin took his $300 and rented an office, put a desk in it, installed a telephone, and cut a deal with a leasing company to rent a helicopter on a per use basis. He was in business.

To attract clients, Robin advertised in the newspaper, stuck flyers under the windshield wipers of cars parked at the airport, and spread the word to students who had flown with him at his old job. Robin also did promotional stints at air shows, showed little kids his helicopter for free, and boldly approached reporters at these events to tell them about Bravo. He knocked a few bucks off his fees for flight lessons and asked that students prepay so that he would have working capital. "Ninety percent of marketing is perception," says Robin. "People want a deal." Robin's approach proved effective. Bookings leapt upward as students came running. Word got out that Bravo was the place to go for flight lessons. "It was just a helicopter and me," says Robin, who has logged over 8,000 hours of flying time. "But I'm a good pilot with a good reputation and that spread by word of mouth."

While revenues grew, the expansion of the business had more to do with Robin's spur-of-the-moment, seemed-like-a-good-idea-at-the-time form of decision making than foresight and business plan implementation. For example, Bravo is also a super-stretch limousine service and car rental agency. Both innovations were Robin-inspired impulses. As the helicopters were parked so far away from the office, he felt he needed transportation to get people to and from the field, so he went to an auction, bid on a limousine, and got it. People started requesting limousine service to and from the airport, and the limousine became a money-making venture.

> *Robin thrives on challenge. His life philosophy is summed up not by "what if?" but by "why not?"*

It also helps that Robin offers a service that is more typically found in Hawaii or Las Vegas: helicopter touring. With a dearth of competitors and California being a hot vacation spot, there is a built-in market for Bravo to tap. Robin's helicopter sight-seeing tours are now part of pre-sold packages offered by travel agencies. (The limousine proved useful again, coming in handy to shuttle clients to and from the commercial airport.) The car rental portion of the business had a similar beginning. Bravo offers lodging for students who come for intensive lessons. Because they often need ground transportation, Robin thought a car rental service wasn't a bad idea. Unfortunately, "car rental was a mistake," he says. "But I went into it to help a friend. I thought I'd take a couple of cars off this friend's hands." The rental business is profitable now but originally was more trouble than it was worth. It started with Robin buying some old cars to shuttle European flight training students who didn't have cars and couldn't rent them without U.S. driver's licenses. The cars broke down on a regular basis, and he pumped a lot of money into the junkers before he realized he'd better buy some reliable vehicles.

Whether it's a roaring success or just a mediocre business decision, Robin accepts the outcome with equanimity. His irrepressible humor bobs to the surface in all manner of circumstances, including those which would cause many people to lose their cool in one way or another. For example, Robin relishes the stories about people who meet him for the first time and discover, with ever-deepening dismay, that he is about to take them up in a helicopter. "Are you going to be the pilot?" is a question that he has been asked more than once by nervous passengers who have never before seen a black pilot. His fairly standard response is, "I don't know if I can fly this thing, but I always wanted to— let's see." His passengers' doubts and fears don't anger or bother him, in part because he is so good at what he does and the people he works with are so proud of him. That support goes a long way.

> *The fact that Robin is both a great helicopter pilot and black elicits a lot of media attention, which is all the better for his business.*

The fact that he is both a great helicopter pilot and black elicits a lot of attention from the media, which is all the better for Bravo. "A lot of news programs like to come out here because they've heard there's a brother who can fly the hell out of a helicopter," he remarks.

Tricks of the Trade

ROBIN'S reputation as a flying phenomenon precedes him in the arena of television and movies as well. A member of the Screen Actors

Guild since 1979, he has acted in films, TV shows, and commercials and now enjoys the opportunity to showcase his aerial photography and stunt flying skills in the same medium. Currently with over thirty music video, television, and film credits to his name (including recent music videos for Brian McKnight, hot director Billy Woodrow, and artist Chico DeBarge), he is in ever-growing demand. Robin brings fresh and original ideas to his film work and is capable of visualizing and performing with ease any maneuver a helicopter can manage.

He is a precision flyer and a master of the one-take scene, skills he demonstrated while flying the camera for the aerial shots in the adventure movies *Eraser* and *Love Kills.* In the action film *Broken Arrow,* he flew the ill-fated red, white, and blue helicopter that chases star John Travolta across the desert before meeting its demise in a fiery explosion. Robin recently wowed a skeptical crew on the set of Lionel Martin's new film, *Jack of All Trades,* by landing the helicopter where no one thought possible, doing it not once but eight times in succession without an error, even after it grew dark. At the end of the day, the performance elicited a standing ovation from the crew.

"Working with productions is what I do best," says Robin, who often makes suggestions that directors love and use. "I can think three-dimensionally to incorporate the director's or producer's vision and get the really unique angles." He likes working with young producers and directors best because they're going to be the next big money guys and hopefully they'll remember Robin when that time comes.

*R*obin wowed a skeptical movie crew by landing a helicopter where no one thought possible—not once but eight times.

With all the stories in the news recently about plane and helicopter crashes of routine flights, is Robin worried about safety in his stunt flying? Robin says no, and adds that safety is always his first consideration. And he only goes along with the use of the term "stunt flying" because everyone understands it. In actuality, he dislikes the term because it suggests a certain recklessness that he would never allow. "All of my maneuvers are well thought out and preplanned with plenty of opportunities to abort if necessary," he says. "I know helicopters well and I know their limitations. There is no guesswork."

Robin is conscious of the value of life and its fleeting nature. His only brother died a few years ago from a stomach infection, which heightened that awareness in Robin. "Life is precious," he says.

From the Screen to the Air

ROBIN'S sense of ease on and off camera comes naturally. He was a stage actor in college at the University of Connecticut and, when he graduated in 1985, moved to New York City to follow the path of most actors, who end up in New York at some point in their career. He thought acting was his calling, but it was not to be.

"I walked holes in my shoes in New York going to auditions," says Robin. "And I couldn't buy a job."

He had known poor and was tired of it. Born in 1962 in Savannah La Mar, Jamaica, Robin lived his first four years in a house without electricity or running water. When he was ten years old, his mother packed up her five children and emigrated to America, to Belmont, Massachusetts, which she chose at random. She worked as a nurse's aide, often day and night, to support her family.

Robin remembers not always being a model kid, until he, typically for him, just decided to change. "In Jamaica, we were so dirt poor that there was no Christmas, no birthdays, or anything like that," he recalls. "But when I got here, people were so nice to me that I tried to learn from that. Besides, being bad was too easy, so I chose to be good."

Ever the contrarian, a hallmark of his life has been to choose the difficult over the easy and then psych himself up for whatever he has already hopped into feet first. That's how he became a candidate for the qualifying rounds in the Olympics. He started running track in high school and says that he used to look at the fastest of his opponents and talk himself into winning. He calls the technique "Petgrave logic."

"People would ask me if I could beat the guy and I would say, 'I don't know.' But I would size the guy up and say to myself, 'He doesn't look faster than me.' Soon I'd have myself believing I could beat him. No matter how much it hurt me, I figured it hurt him a little more and that gave me the edge to win."

From the time Robin was a kid, he yearned to fly, but he thought he had to join the military to learn how.

This method of psychological preparation carried him from New York to Los Angeles in an effort to break into film and television. Throughout the 1980s, he did admirably well as a paid actor, starring in several national commercials for Pepsi, McDonald's, and Taco Bell and landing television roles in *Fame, Spenser: For Hire, The Equalizer,* and the old Nell Carter sitcom, *Gimme a Break.* But his real dream was to fly.

While Robin loves acting, it was not until he discovered that he could be a pilot without compulsory military service that he found his true purpose. From the time he was a kid, he had yearned to fly but had always labored under the misconception that he had to join the military to learn how. "I said, 'I can't do that, I don't look good in green,'" he jokes.

But in 1989, he took a chartered helicopter ride over New York City and got to talking with the pilot, who looked very young. Robin said he figured the guy had to have been barely out of junior high when he entered the army in order to have become a pilot at such a tender age. When the guy told him he had simply taken flying lessons to become certified, Robin was floored. And overjoyed. He signed up for lessons right away.

"All my life I've been doing all these different things," he says. "But when I started flying, nothing else mattered. I stopped working out. I stopped playing sports." He completed a year and a half of flight training at Watson Helicopters and went on to the job he would eventually quit in a fit of justified pique.

Flying is an apt metaphor for everything that makes Robin Petgrave happiest. It allows him a freedom that a desk job could never deliver, and he can play different roles within the construct of the business—teaching and managing as well as flying.

His flying ability is a great equalizer. He cannot count the number of times he has "met" people over the phone only to be greeted with that all-too-familiar look of complete surprise when they actually come face-to-face. "I get a lot of 'Uh . . . you look a lot different than you sound on the phone.' And I say, 'Yeah, I'm a lot . . . taller than I sound on the phone.' A lot of production crews are surprised to see me," he adds, but "aviation levels the playing field. If you can fly, you can fly."

Although Robin flies both planes and helicopters, he prefers the latter because they are tactile machines, more responsive to touch and maneuvering than planes, which are flown by instrument and autopilot. "Flying a helicopter is like driving a stick[shift]; flying a plane is like driving an automatic," he explains. Then he adds with a laugh, "You don't have to finish high school to fly [a helicopter], but you do have to be coordinated."

Talking to kids is important to Robin. "Maybe it'll make a difference and one of them will go on to do better than I did."

Spreading the Joy

BECAUSE he loves flying so much, it is a gift he would like to give to potential pilots. With this in mind, in the summer of 1999, he established the Torrance Aeronautical Museum, a nonprofit organization that he envisions as part flight training school and part historical journey through aviation. The museum will offer exhibitions of antique aircraft and sponsor airplane and helicopter rides for kids, and, although the details are still being worked out, the museum board wants to establish an Aviation Explorers program, which would provide scholarships for high school graduates to attend flight training school or college. But the main idea of the museum is to encourage interest in the field of aviation.

Robin likes kids and makes talking with them, teaching them, and just being there for them a big part of his busy life. "No one did it for me, so I want to do it for others. And maybe it'll make a big difference and one of these kids will go on to do better than I did," Robin says. "Besides, I don't have any kids of my own, so I can spoil somebody else's." Children's drawings paper his office, with those waiting to be hung covering the floor.

Parents often appeal to Robin for help with difficult kids and he takes time out for each and every one. Bravo's "Positive Vibrations Program," a mentoring-by-example project in public and private schools in the Los Angeles area, enables Robin to interact with kids on an individual level and actually get to know some of them. He takes his helicopters and limousines to the schools he visits so the kids can see what he does for a living and learn that there are options out there they may not have even considered. He maintains that his visits have had a positive impact and he has become an inspiration to some children—not just because he's successful, but because he talks to them about their feelings and concerns. Perhaps most important, Robin listens, engaging the kids and helping them to figure out their own solutions for their problems, rewarding them with praise and gifts when they keep their promises to do better in school or to get along at home.

Robin relates one anecdote about a boy named Angel, who was growing up to be a typical L.A. gangbanger. He had already gone along for the ride in a drive-by shooting. When they met, Angel was angry and defiant, determined to be unimpressed by Robin or his helicopter. His first words to Robin were, "You ain't shit!" When Robin asked what he meant, Angel responded, "I can be you!" To which Robin answered calmly, "Yes, you can." They were able to really talk after that and Robin assured Angel that he could be anything he wanted to be, as long as he stayed in school, got an education, and learned to value his life and the lives of others. The last time Robin checked, Angel was still in school and had become a teacher's aide.

"Kids need to generate self-esteem from within," observes Robin. "I got Angel to believe in himself and that he can do things he's not supposed to be able to do." He adds, "Even Michael Jordan didn't make his high school varsity team the first time out, but the coach worked with him."

> "*All you gotta do is figure out what you like and figure out how to make people pay you for it. That's all an entrepreneur is.*"

Robin's work with children is an effort to give them more information than he had growing up, a chance to know that they can do any number of things no one has told them it is okay to pursue. In the course of their interactions, he imparts the usual warnings against drugs and gangs, but he also eases some of the pressure they feel about their futures by telling them they don't have to be scared of not knowing what they want to be when they grow up.

"It'll come to you," he says, which is a pretty fair assessment of how it happened for him.

From Here

BRAVO is growing rapidly right now and Robin is trying to organize, delegate, and manage this growth stage, which he acknowledges can be a dangerous time for a company, especially one that has the potential to double or triple its revenues. Wisely, he is seeking advice from

people more experienced than he in running a multimillion-dollar enterprise and, although the company has been self-financed up until
now, he's considering outside investors.

Although he started Bravo on a wing and a prayer, he realizes it
needs stable and long-sighted guidance from here on. While he now
appreciates the necessity of working with experienced business man-
agers, he has no regrets about the precipitous nature of his initial
jump into Bravo. His message to future entrepreneurs is simple and
to the point: "All you gotta do is figure out what you like and figure
out how to make people pay you for it. That's all an entrepreneur is."

CHAPTER 5

From the Universe to Omniverse

Myra Peterson
President and CEO
Omniverse Digital Solutions, LLC
Springfield, Virginia

Founded: 1997
Number of Employees: 20
Initial Investment: $500,000

MYRA PETERSON LOOKS nothing like the classic techno-geek: no pocket protector, no heavy black frame glasses held together with Scotch tape, no high-water pants, no testosterone. But beneath her sleek, fashion-model exterior beats the heart of a technological wizard with a brain hard-wired for business.

Myra, thirty-seven, is the founder, president, and CEO of Omniverse Digital Solutions, LLC, creators of animation, special effects, and interactive software for television, film, and commercial projects. Omniverse specializes in digital computer technology such as that which brought the movie *Titanic* to life. It also provides production and technological development services to corporate, government, and nonprofit industries

"If you can dream it," says Myra, with a wide grin that shows off a mouth full of braces, "we can do it." As she told *The Conduit,* a newsletter geared to high-tech African Americans, "Behind all the funky images is a lot of technology. Our specialty is creating something that exists only in the minds of our clients. We love being visionary with innovative graphics and technology."

Myra is truly a visionary. The company has myriad cutting-edge projects in the works. Shortly, via e-commerce, broad-band, and Internet technologies, Omniverse will offer an expanded array of products of interest to African Americans and anybody else who wants to go along for the ride.

Dubbed Urbanrepublic.com, or UR, the new Internet-based "cyber mall" will be the first culturally relevant Internet shopping site targeted to the unique buying habits, preferences, and lifestyles of African Americans. From wedding cake toppers to the latest music to the latest news from Africa, it will be available on UR. Urbanrepublic.com will serve not only the black consumer, but also the global "urban" market, which is not limited by race and feeds an ever-widening demand for black music, art, literature, movies, fashion, products, and services.

Nearing the end of its third year, Omniverse is a multimillion-dollar enterprise. More precise figures are unavailable as the company prepares to shift its focus to the Internet-based e-commerce venture. Omniverse is headed by a star-studded cadre of talent including Marc Hannah, who in 1982 co-founded Silicon Graphics, Inc. (SGI), which produced the computers used to create the special effects in *Star Wars, Jurassic Park,* and *Independence Day.*

At the center of it all is Ms. Peterson.

Although she is one of those enviable people who is good at everything—a premier athlete, a brilliant student, an artist, a classically trained pianist—computers are what captured her fascination. "Being black and female and into computers was really crazy, and it set me apart," says Myra, who, at the age of twelve, built her first computer with her electrical engineer father in the basement of their home. But she was also driven by an intense need to create.

> *"If you can dream it, we can do it. Our specialty is creating something that exists only in the minds of our clients."*

"There was always technology and always art," she states. Myra holds both a bachelor's degree in computer science from the University of California, Davis, and a diploma in art history from Richmond College in London, England, along with the firm belief that the two are not really that different. "It's all a creative process. If I can imagine it, I can draw it. If I can draw it, I can make it work," she says, referring to her ability to create software. Omniverse is ultimately the product of a marriage between her two loves, art and technology, and the culmination of a career that began near the top.

Independence, Growth, and Grace Under Pressure

MYRA Peterson started on the road to entrepreneurship as a marketing executive at computer giant Hewlett Packard (HP) in 1984, a good training ground for a woman who would need later in her career both to understand rapidly innovative and changing technology and to know how to sell it. She started at HP right out of college and, during her eight-year tenure there, also served as sales representative and was ranked number three in worldwide sales in the HP minicomputer and workstation divisions. Myra was fortunate in the people she worked

Freedom was a double-edged sword: she was free to make her own choices, but also free to make her own mistakes.

with as well. The man who hired her at Hewlett Packard, Ken Coleman (now a senior vice president at SGI), became a role model, mentor, source of inspiration, and valued friend.

But the siren call of a self-directed creative enterprise eventually lured the Philadelphia-born, California-reared Myra away from her secure position at HP. Although Myra had the job, the six-figure salary, and a company car, she didn't feel fulfilled professionally. She had always yearned to be independent, to own her own business, to push herself, to challenge her abilities. The chance to strike out on her own came when she was offered an opportunity to direct sales and marketing for Lady Nautilus fitness centers. Myra seized the opportunity and even invested her own money in the venture.

Although she was finally free, freedom was a double-edged sword: she was free to make her own choices, but also free to make her own mistakes, which had both career and personal consequences. She discovered that, even in the era of ruthless corporate downsizing, the life of an entrepreneur is much more difficult and far less certain than that of an executive in the lushly carpeted halls of Fortune 500 America.

"That corporate personality is hard to drop," says Myra, who, in the beginning, had a hard time adjusting to a life that required rigorous fiscal discipline. "You're comfortable, you're not accountable 24-7. You can delegate. But an entrepreneur is accountable 24 hours a day.

And it was painful, worrying about rent, the phone, electricity. You're always closer than you think to being homeless."

Myra lost money on the Lady Nautilus investment and, in the process, learned to scale back her lifestyle significantly. For example, when her car broke down, she could not afford to get it fixed. Her parents offered to buy her a new one, but Myra recognized this as the time to stand on her own. She was appreciative of the offer but refused their help. "I said, 'This is character-building time,'" recalls Myra, a fervent believer in self-reliance. Entrepreneurship taught her to be frugal—and how to use public transportation. But her perception of the car debacle reveals one of the keys to her success. Myra chose to view the experience as a challenge, not as defeat. She believes that the point is to judge each obstacle, mistake, or setback on its merits as a learning experience. "It's like a baby learning to walk," she says. "How many times do they fall? But they always get back up."

Standing Tall

THIS ability to stand still, take stock, and then move on is a valuable asset, and one that is essential given the inevitable obstacles black entrepreneurs face, especially as blacks and women move into the business and entrepreneurial world in greater numbers. As recent highly publicized incidents of corporate racism and sexism indicate—the Texaco and Mitsubishi cases, to name two—increasing ranks of women and blacks in the professional world is no guarantee that familiarity breeds less contempt. "I've encountered a lot of racism," Myra says, adding sardonically, "I'm either a jungle bunny or a sex object."

Although people try to squeeze her into their preconceptions, Myra refuses to fit. She has learned how to handle it by staying focused on her goals for herself and for her business. "You put up filters and a lot of people fall away. I've dealt with people who probably wear sheets at night, but I force them to respect me as a woman and an African American."

She has had a lot of practice.

During her days at Hewlett Packard, her legend grew as she gained an industry-wide reputation for excellence based partially on a marketing program she developed to boost corporate sales. At a cocktail party she hosted for an executive group attending one of her seminars, she was introduced to a Boeing executive who knew her by reputation only.

Entrepreneurship taught her how to be frugal— and how to use public transportation.

When he saw she was African American, he was by quick turns surprised, dismissive, and rude. He said that she could not be "the" Myra Peterson, implying that such was impossible, a bad and unfunny joke. His attitude all but screamed, you're black, you're trespassing, get off my patch. Myra's response was to maintain a steely calm. "I told him that Hewlett Packard promotes on the basis of merit, and hopefully after two days with me, he would understand why I have this [position]." Two days later, he apologized and offered her a job.

Her deft handling of the situation stems from lessons she internalized long ago when she was little more than a baby. Myra remembers a teacher from her early years who treated her with similar loathing, a maliciousness so strong it almost radiated heat. This teacher purposely ignored her when she raised her hand in class and underestimated her skill in math and English because it did not fit with her belief that black children could not learn—even though this particular child later brought in computer-related creations for her science projects while other kids arrived with rock gardens.

"I could feel [the teacher's contempt], but I couldn't quite articulate it," says Myra, who came to understand it better as she grew older and recognized that racism is without reason and arbitrarily excludes some while favoring others.

"I remember as a child driving down the street in the car with my mother. We were going to the hardware store and had to pass a country club where all the people I went to school with were allowed to swim [and I was not]. My mom asked me what I wanted from the hardware store and I said 'paint, because I want to paint myself white.'" Her mother laughed and told her that would never work but gave her a priceless piece of advice: "Just be you, and whatever you do be the very best at it."

Racism affects people in different ways. Its hits some with a paralyzing power that destroys self-worth, ambition, and the ability to move beyond its grasp. It could have had the same impact on Myra Peterson but for her mother's words and the love of her family. "My parents are my heroes," she says proudly. "And family is the center of our lives."

Her parents came of age in a world where segregation dominated and restricted all aspects of black life, not the least of which were the professional options open to people of color. Both her mother and father, according to Myra, possessed an unfulfilled desire to own a successful business, a fallen torch that Myra lifted to carry in their honor.

Nevertheless, they set a wonderful example for their children. As an electrical engineer, Myra's father quietly became a self-made millionaire by working hard and saving about every dime he ever made. "My dad is a genius," Myra says with pride. Her mother went from being a licensed cosmetician to working retail to becoming one of the premier disk drive specialists in Silicon Valley. They demonstrated by example how racism can be confronted and conquered. They pushed education, exposed their children to the arts

> *M*yra's mother gave her a priceless piece of advice: "Just be you, and whatever you do be the very best at it."

and sciences, and urged them to excel in school, but they also talked and listened and were Myra's greatest advocates and a source of unconditional love. As a result, Myra grew up believing that she was special and developed an inner strength bolstered by her strong support system. This combination gives her confidence that she can meet whatever lies ahead.

On Her Own

AFTER Hewlett Packard and Lady Nautilus, Myra Peterson's professional life took an upward turn in the form of Krysp Imaging Solutions. Under her direction as co-founder and vice president, the company became one of the leading resellers for SGI's high-end computer equipment in the San Francisco area, which facilitated Myra becoming a long-term management consultant for Silicon Graphics.

Anxious to use more of her creative talents, in 1995, she left Krysp Imaging Solutions and co-founded Digital Universe Organization, LLC, a multimedia development and management consulting company. The move allowed her to move beyond hardware to developing all kinds of software and online content. Myra also was able to combine her eight years of HP management, sales experience, and training with her small business management experience gained at Krysp to assist other companies in building and increasing their operations.

In her consulting capacity at DUC, she continued working with SGI, fashioning new strategies to expand their entertainment market. Myra was also instrumental in the launch of the SGI subsidiary Silicon Studio, a top provider of computer and related software to the entertainment community. She helped create marketing programs for Michael Jackson, the Rolling Stones, David Bowie, and Sinbad and developed the successful SGI-sponsored annual technology summit conference for African American leaders in the technology and entertainment fields. The conference provides technologists and those in the entertainment industry an opportunity to meet and exchange ideas about how they can work together for mutual benefit.

The conference presented Myra with yet another business opportunity. While leading one of the SGI-sponsored workshops at the annual conference, Myra so impressed actor-producer Tim Reid (best known for his critically acclaimed television series *Frank's Place*) with her knowledge of media technology that he invited her to oversee technology development for his new multimillion-dollar film studio, New Millennium, in Virginia. This would involve supervising systems building for a variety of functions including film editing, graphic design, and animation. Myra half-jokingly said "sure," and put it out of her mind.

But the Reids were serious about her building their technological capacity. They made the offer in June 1997, and by November Myra and partners had made a decision to dissolve Digital Universe, and she had incorporated Omniverse Digital Solutions. The Reids persisted and, in May 1998, Myra moved permanently to Petersburg, Virginia. Soon after, the New Millennium studio broke ground.

The Reids' offer was not only too good to pass up; it put Myra in the right place at the right time. In 1997, Washington, D.C./Virginia was solidifying its reputation as "Silicon Valley East," with the explosion of technology behemoth America Online and various other fast-growing tech companies headquartered in the area. As Myra told *Black Enterprise* magazine, "This is where innovation is happening. There are large and small computer hardware, software, and Internet companies all mixed together fostering creativity."

In addition to professional satisfaction and Omniverse, Virginia had other compensations for Myra. A few months after moving to Petersburg, Myra met her future fiancé. The appropriately named Eric Love happened to live in the same building, and they became friends. The relationship was solid from the first and Eric is now Myra's partner at home and in business. Although he is nearly ten years younger than she, he is no less mature for his youth. He is clearly as devoted to her as she is to him. "I take care of her so she can take care of business," says Love. "I cook . . ." he begins the sentence, and Myra finishes it, ". . . and I clean."

Eric, who works as an assistant comptroller for a Virginia-based company, is in his own right a bit of a technical guru (Myra declares he's on the genius track, too). He has learned enough about computers, networking, and software to act as Myra's systems troubleshooter and advisor in his spare time. He always had a yen for things technical but was discouraged from pursuing his dream to become an engineering major in college. In that sense, his involvement in Omniverse has fulfilled his dreams too. But only in part. His real coup is Myra. "We have a great relationship," says Eric. "We talk about everything, but we don't take business home."

Trust Your Instincts

SOON they may have to break that rule. Omniverse is at a critical juncture. The company has been experiencing growth pangs recently and is moving rapidly away from doing solely business-to-business transactions to releasing products and offering new services directly to the consumer market, via e-commerce. Direct distribution to consumers of products such as music opens up new possibilities for those who have no access to traditional media. The objective is to "free African American stories that don't get told," explains Myra. To that end, she is also considering a huge move to launch a broad-band network that would allow users to download movies and television programs at any time.

This type of major expansion requires serious capital. Until now, Omniverse has been self-financed and carries no debt. Myra has put her money back into the business and, like many young millionaires, she doesn't work for the money; the money works for her. That same sage financial acumen will guide her plans for business expansion. New media- and technology-based businesses are such a hot investment commodity right now that people are literally lined up to capitalize Omniverse. Myra is carefully considering with whom she wants to form strategic alliances and who she will allow to invest in the company. It is vital, she says, to pick your business partners and investors with great care. "I've had good business partners and bad ones. If there's someone who doesn't treat people right that tells me something," she says. If Myra has any advice for young people looking to succeed, it is: "Trust your instincts and don't hesitate to use them in business."

The Booming African American Market

OMNIVERSE recently wrapped an independent film by Eagle Films due out next year and is producing a number of CD-ROMs with content ranging from multicultural children's fables and stories to art for adults. Arguably, their most fascinating venture, in partnership with a leading university, is an interactive program called "Virtual Harlem." The program allows the user to transport him- or herself back in time to 1920s Harlem, where one can hear back-to-Africa black nationalist Marcus Garvey preach self-determination or enter the Cotton Club to hear Duke Ellington play or see Josephine Baker dance the Black Bottom. The program allows the user to pick his or her identity, and the Harlem experience is different depending on the race, age, and gender of the visitor. For example, if the user chooses to identify as an African American and approaches the front door of the Cotton Club, the doorman will tell him or her to stop and go around to the back—just as doormen did at the actual club in the 1920s.

> *M*yra's advice for young people looking to succeed is: "Trust your instincts and don't hesitate to use them in business."

Myra is convinced that the market is hungry for such unique material. "The big guys [such as Disney and Microsoft] don't believe there's a market for these products, but I know it's there," she says, adding that the market is also broader, deeper, and more diverse than white companies assume.

The truth, she says—and she is right, if popular culture is any indication—is that black products attract consumers across the racial spectrum. For too long, larger media technology producers have looked at black products and content as something only a black audience would want to buy. And since they feel blacks have little interest in technology, it follows that they believe there is no market for those products. Not so, declares Myra. Look at music, listen to how we speak, look at what white kids in the suburbs are wearing. "White people buy black culture," she says.

> *The truth is that black products attract consumers across the racial spectrum. White people buy black culture.*

Quiet as the fact is kept, black people also buy computers and related products. In 1997, according to *Target Market News,* African Americans bought about $751 million worth of computers, technological equipment, and software. And they are outpacing white consumers by about two-to-one in online service subscriptions.

Myra and Omniverse plan to be there to meet the needs of the booming African American market as well as the market in general.

Helping Others Succeed

BUSINESS success is a goal, but not Myra's only motivation. She is devoted to providing more young people of color entrée to learning opportunities in technology. In addition to its educational material for children and adolescents, Omniverse has developed an internship program to help students build the skills and knowledge necessary to become proficient and competitive in an increasingly technology-oriented job market.

Last year, Omniverse held its first technological conference in Virginia, focused on internship outreach to students who attend historically black colleges, Hispanic-serving colleges, and tribal (Native American) colleges. Omniverse interns do everything from answering telephones to helping brainstorm concepts for new projects. They get invaluable on-the-job experience in digital media production (CDs, virtual reality development, and two- and three-dimensional animation), media technology development (hardware and software development, network and systems integration), and media technology management (market studies, consulting services, and project management).

> *"We won't be satisfied until you can walk into every African American home and there's a computer in the house."*

Former intern Troy Benjamin, a graduate of South Carolina State University, said in an interview that he values the real, behind-the-scenes, hands-on experience he got at Omniverse. "I [interned] because I wanted to learn the not-so-glamorous side of moviemaking. It's a great picture out front, but in the background, it's a lot of hard work."

It is part of Myra Peterson's mission to make technology less formidable and more user friendly for everybody, but particularly for the underexposed African American student and the long-ignored, underserved black consumer market.

"We won't be satisfied," says Myra, "until you can walk into every African American home and there's a computer in the house, because the Internet, technology, represents freedom." For Myra, technology is not just about making money, it is a critical educational tool and something African Americans must understand and become adept at using in order to progress and flourish in the next century. She is applying her multitude of skills and a determination that recognizes no barriers to help make this happen.

CHAPTER **6**

Ciao, Baby!

Todd B. Alexander
Managing Director
Vendemmia, Inc.
Atlanta, Georgia

Founded: 1994
1998 Revenues: Over $1 million
Number of Employees: 7
Initial Investment: $50,000
Net Worth: $1.5 million

Vines love an open hill.

—Virgil

HOW DOES AN average upper-middle-class brother from Atlanta, Georgia, become fluent in Italian, a connoisseur of Italian wine, and the founder of a multimillion-dollar wine distribution company?

"I like to eat," says Todd B. Alexander matter-of-factly. He is serious. Since childhood, Todd, thirty-one, has gravitated toward the kitchen, always anticipating his next meal and looking for the source of the tantalizingly rich aromas wafting from pots simmering on the stove. His family traveled a fair amount both in the United States and abroad and Todd came to love the excitement of sampling the culture and cuisine of different regions and countries. He jokes that on their frequent trips, his parents would often look up from the table in a restaurant to find Todd missing. They could usually find him in the kitchen, standing next to the chef, watching with intense fascination the preparation of breakfast, lunch, or dinner.

It is a small leap from a love affair with food to one with wine, according to Todd. "Wine is considered food in Europe," he says. "A good wine can make a great meal spectacular."

In an effort to share that simple discovery with the world, and in particular the African American community, Todd Alexander founded Vendemmia, Inc., the only black-owned wine distribution company in operation today. Based in his native Atlanta, Vendemmia (Italian for "harvest") brought in revenues of over $1 million in 1998.

While Todd could have predicted that he would own his own business one day, he never imagined that he would become an oenophile, a lover of wine, so enthralled with the fruit of the grape that he would dedicate his career to it. Scion of a long line of businessmen and businesswomen—his grandfather owned an insurance company and his father was an investment banker and the first black stockbroker in the Southeast—Todd inherited the entrepreneurial spirit and a strong work ethic. His business is housed in a building owned by his family on historic Auburn Avenue in Atlanta, once a center of African American commerce. Generations may have handed down the entrepreneurial mantle to Todd, but the discriminating palate and devotion to wine are entirely of his own cultivation.

Todd, who is easygoing and as mellow as a southern afternoon, is impatient with pretense (especially pretensions about wealth) and is not driven by celebrity, ego, or money. "There are easier ways to earn money," he says. "But as I always tell people, you have to be in it for something other than money." The strongest motivation for Todd is freedom, which means flexibility in his personal and professional life and generous down time for leisure. He wants to enjoy his life to the fullest extent before he shuffles off this mortal coil, so he made it his business to find a career that would cater to his loves, one that would give him the freedom to travel abroad, eat good food, and drink exquisite wine.

Vendemmia is a small adventure at the beginning of what Todd hopes will be a long and interesting ride through life.

The result is Vendemmia, which represents over one hundred wineries around the world, including ones in Italy, France, New Zealand, California, Washington State, and Oregon, and specializes in the lesser-known and less-celebrated but excellent Italian wines, such as the barolos, chiantis, barbarescos, and valpolicellas. Although Todd believes that Italian wines can stand up to any competition, including to the more well known French varieties, Italian wines are largely unknown commodities on this side of the Atlantic.

Vendemmia sells mainly to bars, restaurants, hotels, and other outlets that buy wholesale; among its clients are the Ritz Carlton, Bacchanalia restaurant, and Ansley Wine Merchants. However, the company also sponsors tastings in an effort to introduce individual consumers to the wines from countries other than France.

According to Todd, Vendemmia goes out of its way to make wine buying a convenient and pleasant experience. For example, clients do not pay extra for ordering individual bottles (they pay the same price whether they buy one bottle or fifty cases), and every other Monday, clients can get same-day delivery within fifty miles of Atlanta, Savannah, and all cities in between. The company is happy to sponsor tastings and is in the process of building a wine-tasting program. Todd hopes in the future to offer a lecture series to open up the world of wine, a new vista for African Americans to explore.

> *In his Hawaiian print shirt, khakis, and sandals, Todd looks more like a college student than a wine connoisseur.*

The man is almost a walking contradiction: he is an industrious lover of pleasure who works hard so he can fully afford his leisure. In his Hawaiian print shirt, khakis, and sandals, he looks more like a college student than a wine connoisseur. But Todd is living proof that you can find your heart's desire if you search for it and live your dream if you dare.

The Odyssey

IT cannot be said often enough: Todd Alexander is passionate about food. His obsession with it began early, about when he was old enough to peek over the counter to determine what his mother was up to in the kitchen. "I did a lot of watching because I was always hungry," says Todd, laughing.

The youngest son in a family of much older siblings, he developed the introspection and coping skills of the only child early on. He read a great deal, entertained himself with solitary pursuits, and demonstrated the high spirits of a typical kid as well as a penchant for some not-so-typical pursuits. "I played tennis and football and sometimes threw rocks at cars," he says. "I could be a scoundrel."

But while Todd was becoming proficient with a tennis racket and a football, he was also developing skills with a wok and a whisk. In fifth grade, he went to a French cooking school, courtesy of a prize his parents won at an auction, and discovered he loved cooking as much as he loved to eat. His hunger for more diverse knowledge led him in ninth grade to a Chinese cooking school, even as he continued more routine activities. He excelled as a wrestler in high school, ironically the one sport where weight is heavily scrutinized, calculated to the ounce, and always an issue. "Wrestlers can't eat," says Todd. "So I obsessed more about food."

While he maintained his interest in sports, Todd was, in his own words, "not a model student." His creative inclinations drew him away from the ordinary. He did not know exactly what he would do with his life, but he knew that medical or law school were neither plausible nor preferred options. "I wanted to go to college," says Todd, "but people place too much emphasis on grades and not enough on learning."

Clearly, he harbored great enthusiasm for the things he was interested in learning. Toward the end of high school at Atlanta's Westminsters Prep School, he participated in an exchange program and spent a semester in Italy. Todd had already developed a fascination with international travel. His mother worked for the airlines and his father had also been an exchange student, traveling to Russia while in college. His parents' stories fueled Todd's imagination and the fire to experience living abroad.

While Todd was becoming proficient with a tennis racket and a football, he was also developing skills with a wok and a whisk.

During his exchange semester, Todd stayed with an Italian family who treated him like a son. From its luscious green hills to its great historic and cultural centers, the country where Caesar ruled and Carthaginian general Hannibal crossed the Alps to conquer Rome captured his heart.

And of course there was the wine. Italy produces more wine than any country except France and is a prodigious consumer of its product. In Italy, wine flows like water and has traditionally been the customary drink of both peasants and kings. Unlike Europeans, Americans tend to think of good wine as an ornamental drink more suited to celebratory occasions. They are apt to be intimidated by wine's association with refined sippers, as well as by the sheer amount of information involved in distinguishing one wine from another. In Europe, says Todd, he gained a whole new perspective on wine. When he began to drink wine on a regular basis as it is served in Italy, it lost its mythic quality but still intrigued him. What made one wine better than another? What made it different? What influenced the differences?

When Todd returned to the United States, he finished high school and chose to attend Cornell University in Ithaca, New York, where he majored in marketing to learn basic business principles, with the vague notion that he might open a restaurant one day. But he was really unsure about the course he wanted his life to take and spent a semester in college abroad, returning to his beloved Italy in an effort to figure out where he would go.

> "*I* had seen wine imported, distributed, retailed, and talked about, but I had never seen a grape on the vine."

While there, he concentrated on how to create a niche for himself. He had no interest in any career that would require him to go to school for many more years, sit behind a desk eight hours a day, or remain rooted in one spot a moment longer than he felt like being there. He thought about the restaurant, but that would have required him to quell his travel lust for an unforeseeable period of time.

So Todd ruminated while delving more deeply into the mysteries of Italy. "Once I sink my teeth into something, I'm in it," declares Todd. In this case, he immersed himself in Italian culture and attended an Italian language school. He lived in an apartment by himself so that he would have to be independent. In his self-imposed exile from the English-speaking world, Todd became fluent in Italian. He was on a tight budget, so he became an expert on pasta and the surprisingly good wine that can be had for relatively little money in Italy. He read Italian, listened to Italian radio, and perused numerous books on Italian wine, anxious to quench his thirst for knowledge on the subject.

"I was in awe at the variety of Italian wine," he recalls. "And I started wondering what differentiates one from another." With this question, Todd unknowingly took on a huge challenge, one that led him to his chosen career. The question of what distinguishes one wine from another is not simply answered; it is a subject worthy of a lifetime of study. When Todd returned to the United States after his semester in Italy, he brought with him a fire to thoroughly learn wine.

Pursuing a Passion

STILL uncertain about his ultimate destiny, Todd threw himself into his new passion with a vengeance. After college, he went to work for Winebow, Inc., a fine wine importer and distributor located in New Jersey. There he embarked on a long apprenticeship. He began educating his palate by tasting thousands of wines, talked with growers, and immersed himself in all aspects of the business of importing wine and selling it to on-premise servers (restaurants, bars, and hotels).

"It was extremely good experience," says Todd, who left the distributor to work for wine retailer Sherry-Lehmann Wines and Spirits in New York City. There, he worked the floor and the phones and was introduced to a wide spectrum of wines while he gained valuable insight into the buying habits and patterns of the individual consumer. But, to really understand the true nature and distinctions among Italian wines—his first love—he would have to return to Italy.

"I had seen wine imported, distributed, retailed, and talked about, but I had never seen a grape on the vine," he says. "You have to see it, experience it. It's important to be there."

Todd already knew that wine is much more than yeast-fermented grape juice. It is an ancient product, older than recorded time. Although its roots lie in Egypt, the Romans were at the forefront of winemaking. Wine is the result of a creative process refined over centuries by the Greeks, Phoenicians, and Romans. (The latter are actually responsible for planting the vines in what is now modern France, considered by many to produce the best wine in the world—an opinion with which Todd disagrees.) The Italians are the direct descendants of those early winemakers.

Todd returned to Italy with the thought in mind that he wanted to write a book about Italian wine. In order to accomplish this he needed to develop an expertise beyond that of the casually educated wine drinker. Starting at the heel of the boot that is Italy, he drove an old used Fiat from one end of the country to the other, seeking out and speaking to wine growers he thought merited special attention. As he traversed the countryside, he saw for himself the intricate process that defines winemaking, the factors that influence the final product, how critical grapes are to determining the wine's character—from flavor and alcohol content to acidity and color. He found that a wine's character is further shaped by viticultural practices used during the growth process, meaning how vines are trained, trellised, harvested, and pruned.

It was critical for Todd to actually see those processes at work in the environment of the grape's origin. To be truly expert in the field of wine, he needed to understand winemaking from bud to harvest to fermentation to the finished product. He spent nearly every day of four months tasting and observing how natural factors make wine from a specific region unique. Known in the wine industry as *terroir,* these factors include local climate, temperature, rainfall, and sunlight. In the vineyards, Todd could see how altitude and the grade of the slope on which the vines were planted affected their fruit. He could feel the composition of the soil (grapevines grow best in sandy, chalky, rocky soil) and note its ability to drain water.

As he drove from region to region, the book idea became less of an attraction and a new idea took form. He found that a number of

Italian growers were unhappy with their U.S. distribution networks. While the French are lauded for the quality of their wines and are master marketers, according to Todd, Italians wines are as good if not better, but are less well known. Especially in his home city of Atlanta.

"Atlanta was behind the times," says Todd. "But Italian growers were interested in getting into the Atlanta market." Italian growers knew Atlanta because the CNN television network, based there, has made it a globally recognized city and seems intent on proving that Atlanta is as cosmopolitan and sophisticated as any other American metropolis. Atlanta's possibilities as a doorway to an underserved market intrigued Italian growers.

There are only about thirteen licensed liquor distributors in the state of Georgia, with four large firms dominating the business. None specialize to the degree Vendemmia does in Italian wines. Until recently, wine buyers and connoisseurs have not considered Italian wines to be on a par with French offerings. There are differences of opinion as to why, but there seems to be a consensus that the French regulated the winemaking process so as to ensure consistent quality and, until recently, Italy did not. French wines, therefore, have long-established reputations and legions of loyalists.

Italian wines are only now beginning to gain similar respect and notice. While some Italian wine has always had a coterie of fans in northeastern cities like New York and Philadelphia, the southeastern United States re-

> "*No one knew me or the wine. And there were no African Americans in the wine business in Atlanta.*"

mained largely untapped as a serious market for Italian wine until Vendemmia came along. Italian growers recognized the potential for establishing a presence in this virtually virgin territory.

Todd, with his knowledge of both the product and the import, distribution, and retail sale of wine, was uniquely qualified to act as broker and promoter. As he told the *Atlanta Tribune* a couple of years ago,

"This business is all about relationships and it's important for wineries to know what I'm trying to do here. They need my company because I give them a way to market their line and I need them because they give me something to sell. It is a mutually beneficial relationship."

A Business Is Born

ONCE she saw he was serious about wine, his mother loaned him $50,000. Todd bought his first thousand cases of wine and Vendemmia, Inc., was born in January of 1994. But all was not smooth sailing. "No one knew me or the wine," says Todd, recalling his foray into unchartered wine territory in a tough market. "And there were no African Americans in the wine business in Atlanta."

He had an uphill battle to educate consumers, restaurants, and stores about Italian wine. "The variety, the diversity, and the sheer quantity of Italian wine is intimidating," states Todd, and the classification and nomenclature of Italian wine can make it more confusing. "Italians name wine after the region, the grape, the town, their dog," he says, laughingly. There were, in addition, the usual problems associated with bringing a new product to an untried public. Taste is a notoriously fickle quality to judge. Some wine Todd personally liked had little market value. He ended up selling only about sixty-five percent of his original stock, and thirty-five percent sat gathering dust until it became part of Todd's personal collection.

He got a better feel for what would sell by going out and knocking on doors, talking to potential clients about the preferences of the market, educating them about Italian wine, and, of course, letting them sample the products. Todd says he did have doors slammed in his face on occasion, but because he came to the table with quality products, more doors opened than closed. "I let the wine speak for itself," says Todd. And Vendemmia thrived.

Based on his experiences over the past five years, Todd has developed a sanguine attitude about the business. "I've had hits and misses;

there's no science in terms of wine," he says. "The guidelines for the business are to trust your palate and pick your fights." Vendemmia is more select than the other wine distributors in Georgia, according to Todd, and, although the company also sells California and French wine, it is recognized by restaurants, bars, and hotels in Atlanta and the surrounding area as *the* house for Italian wine.

Todd did a three-year plan when he started the business and another after the initial three years were up. Now in his fifth year, he says the biggest challenge is managing and capitalizing the growth and expansion of Vendemmia. He is in the process of developing a good operating system and trying to let go of the reins by allocating more responsibility to his staff of seven. "When I started the business, I did the bookkeeping, delivery, and sales," says Todd, adding, "I have problems delegating."

> *T*odd sets an example for everyone who ever imagined being paid for doing what they loved and was told no, you can't make money, do the sensible/prudent/ commonsense thing.

As for race, it does tend to rear its ugly head in the course of business, Todd reports. For example, he thinks it is interesting that the Georgia Department of Revenue once confiscated his wine at a tasting on a tip from a competitor, something which as far as he knows has never happened to a white distributor. On the other hand, the support of the black community has not always been consistent. He has found it difficult to sell wine to some black outlets because his product is too expensive, and he has encountered some of that not-so-subtle, crabs-in-a-barrel jealousy that seems to accompany success. Todd has little patience for either, and none of it is sufficiently troublesome to stop him.

Leading by Example

TODD Alexander sets an important example for other young entrepreneurs by thinking beyond the reach of the usual. He sets an example for dreamers as well, for every person who ever imagined being paid for doing what they loved and was told no, you can't make money, do the sensible/prudent/commonsense thing. Todd is also a big-picture thinker in terms of economics. The sooner black folks realize that their collective economic power can enhance their political clout, the better off we will be as a people, the better our opportunities to leverage change, he says. "I go to schools to talk to black students about business. I make it a point to put my money in a black bank. I own a business housed in a black-owned building," says Todd. "I want people to say, 'He did a lot for his people.' I would like to be known for bringing some cohesiveness to the structure of black economics."

Another legacy he would like to leave is to endow the next generation of potential African American entrepreneurs with a sense of confidence. "I got my self-confidence from my family," he says, but not all young black kids get that, and they are exposed to a barrage of negative and demeaning media images of African Americans.

Todd believes he has been successful because his family believed in themselves and they passed down to him that entitlement to confidence, the knowledge that you can trust your instincts and abilities. One day, he says, Vendemmia will be all it's ever going to be and he will move on to start another business unrelated to wine, and he still has so much of the world to see and other languages to learn. Vendemmia is a small adventure at the beginning of what he hopes will be a long and interesting ride through life.

"Lifestyle is very important," says Todd, who is unmarried but would like to marry and have a family one day. "I will not work myself into having a heart attack. The journey is as important as the destination. I'm only here once."

Hollywood Shuffle

Takashi Bufford
President and CEO
Kid, I Love It But You'll Never Get It Made, Not In This Town
Los Angeles, California

Founded: 1993
1998 Revenues: $550,000
Number of Employees: 2
Initial Investment: $0
Current Net Worth: $1 million

W E TYPICALLY THINK of writers as tortured, under-
appreciated souls condemned to suffer a life of poverty,
deprivation, and, more often than not, obscurity for the
sake of their craft. Any writer will tell you not to make writing a career unless you are possessed by a fire in your belly and can live without eating regularly. If you want money, be an investment banker. If
you want to create, be a writer.

Takashi Bufford has managed to turn that familiar scenario on its
head to both achieve critical success and reap the financial rewards
from his passion: writing. A lawyer in his first life, Takashi left courts
and torts behind to pursue the muse full-time as a television and film
writer and producer, contriving in the process to make the transition
look seamless.

The company he started in 1993—Kid, I Love It But You'll Never
Get It Made, Not In This Town—is already successful, clearing between $400,000 and $600,000 annually. The company is a writer's
loan-out, meaning a corporation of one formed specifically to do
business with studios and other entities who contract writers. Once
writers, songwriters, or actors begin to earn more than $150,000 a
year, it is common for them to form this kind of corporation. The
company's primary product is Takashi, and it exists to sell his talents
as a writer and producer.

The key to Takashi's success in a difficult industry is due in no
small measure to his ability to reconcile seeming opposites: he considers writing a marriage between business and art. Son of a Japanese
mother and an African American father, Takashi, 46, is a man defined
by contrasts. He lives in the Los Angeles–area beach town of Venice,
in the original Gold's Gym building, site of serious bodybuilding long
before buff became a national obsession. From the outside, his home
looks like an abandoned warehouse. Inside is a spacious loft with
soaring ceilings, tawny hardwood floors polished to a high gloss, and
soft ambient lighting to set off an eclectic modern art collection.
Takashi's name is another study in contrasts and reflects his integra-

tive approach to life and work: "Takashi" suggests lyrical elegance, while "Bufford" evokes rock-solid practicality and dependability.

Blessed with creative ability and having developed a keen knowledge of the television and film business, Takashi is a talented artist who knows his market like a stockbroker knows the Dow. While he does not create art for art's sake ("this is not art, this is show business") he is driven by the love of storytelling, the process of developing and shaping characters, giving them a voice, ushering them through the conflict of drama and the perils of comedy. But he balances that with an eye toward

> *The key to Takashi's success in a difficult industry is due in no small measure to his ability to reconcile seeming opposites: business and art.*

what audiences want, what brings them to the theater, what compels them to tune in to television week after week.

Changing the Face on the Screen

TAKASHI and other African American writers and producers, as well as directors, are changing the face of the filmmaking industry and influencing the market by providing an expanded number of viewing choices. Where pop-eyed, language-mangling, foot-shuffling subservience once defined the range of parts available to black actors, new opportunities, images, and possibilities are slowly emerging. Will Smith in *Men in Black,* Wesley Snipes in *Blade,* and the four fabulous female leads (Whitney Houston, Angela Bassett, Loretta Devine, and Lela Rochon) in *Waiting to Exhale* all suggest that Hollywood is opening its collective mind a crack to enlarge the playing field for black actors, which in turn should open the door a little wider for black writers.

Although no one is predicting an overnight revolution, change prompted by the market and insider pressure is under way. Writer-producers like Takashi have contributed to that elemental change by providing a voice and forum for black characters with a never-before-seen sense of dignity, dimension, and depth. Takashi knows, however, that his personal success is based in large part on his ability to turn out product that turns a profit. "I've never made a movie that didn't make money," says the soft-spoken Takashi, the prolific writer and producer of commercial hits such as *Set It Off,* starring Queen Latifah and Jada Pinkett-Smith, the sex farce *Booty Call,* and the critically acclaimed but short-lived *413 Hope Street* on the FOX network.

> *Takashi and other African American writers and producers are changing the face of the film-making industry.*

Although his projects are made for and marketed to a black audience, that does not mean that Takashi's talent or writing is race specific. But it will take time for Hollywood to discard its traditional mindset that black audiences are homogeneous, says Takashi. The reason is in part that racism limits the thinking of white power brokers in Hollywood and in part that the most reliable, ticket-buying black audiences are the young hip-hoppers who go to see violent, "in the 'hood" movies and shun more cerebral offerings like *Beloved.* The movie and television industry has a ways to go before it considers black artists and films on a par with those deemed "mainstream." But Takashi Bufford intends to keep pushing for change, using his advantage as a man who has magic in his pen and the ability to spin tales that people pay to see.

A Kid with a Dream

IT is hard to imagine Takashi as a lawyer, bent over thick, dusty tomes, writing legal briefs and memoranda of law as dry as toast, because he is happiest when he talks about fiction writing. His voice lifts and he smiles broadly, occasionally letting forth a raucous laugh. Clearly, storytelling is something he loves.

That love began early in Takashi's life. Born in Birmingham, Alabama, he was the middle child in a military family that moved frequently. In the process of all their moves, Takashi learned that stories were completely portable: he could pick them up and carry them with him wherever he went.

Characterizing himself as an uninspired student who got A's when he had to and B's when it was necessary, Takashi resisted spoon-fed knowledge, preferring to concentrate on what he wanted to learn instead of following a decreed course of study. He always took the path of least resistance, he says—except when it came to writing. He was so serious about it that, when he was twelve years old, his parents paid for a correspondence course for writers, even though it was a luxury they could barely afford.

When he was eleven or twelve, on his own initiative, Takashi wrote a script for the 1960s television crime-drama *I Spy*, which starred salt-and-pepper duo Robert Culp and Bill Cosby. "I wrote it longhand and didn't know what to do with it next," recalls Takashi. Although he was motivated to write for black actor Cosby—whose character was smart and strong and seemed to symbolize a coming revolution in black characterizations on television to parallel the civil rights revolution on the street at that time—without a mentor or role models, Takashi was set adrift with no way to nurture his dream of becoming a professional writer.

In the post–civil rights era, according to historians and social observers, black children traditionally were encouraged to go to college, to follow a professional course of study that would guarantee success. Be a doctor, an accountant, an engineer. Do something that promises a steady paycheck and benefits. It was considered extraordinary enough for blacks to reach for professions heretofore mostly closed to their entry. But a writer . . . Even white writers were poor. The prudent choice was the only one that made sense. That logic was little comfort to a young man whose talent lay in exercising his constantly churning imagination, creating characters out of whole cloth.

Takashi was held in thrall to that imagination, making up stories all the time. He humorously recounts how he created a television drama while on his way home from Little League practice one day, a story about three young cops who were pure '70s fiction, young, hip, on the side of the law. Later that summer, Aaron Spelling's *Mod Squad* debuted on television, under the billing "one black, one white, one blonde," one of the first stabs at gender and race equality casting and light-years away from the Jack Webb characterization of the white-socked, black-shoed cop.

> *Without a mentor or role models, Takashi was set adrift with no way to nurture his dream of becoming a professional writer.*

"I felt violated," says Takashi, laughing. "Really. I was angry. But then I thought, 'Damn, I must be good. I want to go to Hollywood.'"

He continued to write but, unsure about how to make that particular leap, did the sensible thing and attended Howard University in Washington, D.C., the city he still considers home even though he now lives three thousand miles away in Los Angeles. He took theater and writing classes, searching for the key to a door he was not at all sure a young black man in the 1970s could unlock. In an attempt to get as close as he dared to the life he really wanted, he went on to law school at the University of California at Los Angeles. Even in the midst of the hellish schedule law school imposes on its prisoners, he kept writing, though no one was reading his work or encouraging him.

The Law and the Leap

TAKASHI'S primary reason for becoming an attorney was that he most emphatically did not want to wait tables in Los Angeles while waiting for his big break. After graduating from law school in 1983, he returned to D.C., where the law welcomed him with open arms. The seduction of a boring but constant lover often breeds complacency. For Takashi, it was easier to live with the certainty than the fear of giving it up to pursue his real passion. Before he knew it, he had been a lawyer for five long years, doing gratifying but not soul-satisfying work.

He worked in various progressive spheres of law, including doing stints with the federally funded Legal Services Corporation, which provides legal assistance to the poor and with D.C.'s public schools. At the time, the District of Columbia had just won the right to limited self-government. It was an exciting time to be in a city whose black population was in the majority and where self-determination had just become a reality. Takashi was able to help young people, which he found rewarding. He even hung his shingle out and tried private practice for a while, but like an insomniac who tosses and turns, he was unable to get comfortable. None of it felt right.

Then one day Takashi woke up and said, "Enough." He knew he had to go full-out for the writing, he recalls. "It was now or never. So I took the mental leap." While he would not quit the law completely till 1992, he dedicated himself to writing as he had not since becoming a lawyer. He wrote screenplay after screenplay and sent out three or four over the next seven years, none of which elicited a response. But he was doing what all real writers do: they write far more than they publish or sell and they do it day in and day out. The point is to improve storytelling and writing skills, and the only way to accomplish that is to write. Real writers also do it because they love it, and many do it for themselves alone, never sharing with the rest of the

> *T*akashi's primary reason for becoming an attorney was that he most emphatically did not want to wait tables in Los Angeles while waiting for his big break.

world what they've created. Takashi loved it, but he wanted to make a career of it as well. In 1990, he finally got his big break.

Production companies, studios, some agents, and scriptwriter's programs accept material submitted by new writers (some can be found through the Writer's Guild–West or in writer's guides available at bookstores). By this time, Takashi had conducted a self-taught course in how to submit pieces for Hollywood review, and he sent his latest film script (a psychological thriller about a black D.C. homicide cop on the trail of a psychopathic killer compulsively drawn to commit multiple murders in the same building) to Disney, which sponsors a prestigious writer's development workshop. It got a look and, happily, they offered him a contract for $30,000.

After long years of dedicated service to his craft, he was a paid writer, though not well paid by industry standards and, as far as he was concerned, not paid enough to quit his job in D.C. Wisely (he admits he was also scared), knowing the vagaries of Hollywood, Takashi became bi-coastal, flying to Los Angeles and back to Washington an exhausting average of twice a month. His Disney fellowship was renewed in 1991 and he maintained that pace until 1992, when he made the permanent move to the West Coast to become a full-time writer.

It so happened that at that time opportunities for black writers and actors were opening up as Hollywood experienced one of its periodic waves of expansiveness. A flurry of movies by innovative, young black filmmakers (Spike Lee, John Singleton, Matty Rich, the Hudlin brothers), the heavily anticipated *Waiting to Exhale,* and the new incarnation of blaxploitation films, or violence verité aimed at the hip-hop generation, made studios scramble for stories geared to the African American market.

Takashi sold *Set It Off* and *Booty Call* on spec, meaning he wrote the scripts without getting paid, and was lucky enough to sell both to studios. Both were made into movies and both received respectable reviews, although the process of making a script into a movie is a little like making sausage, he claims—you really don't want to know what goes into it. In the case of *Set It Off,* only about fifty percent of his script made it into the movie. The rest was the director's vision of the film.

According to Takashi, his version of *Set It Off,* the story of four African American childhood friends who are victimized by the system and turn to robbing banks as a way of extracting their own brand of justice, was more nuanced and less violent, with more fully drawn characters, than what eventually made it onto the big screen. Although he could have been happier with the final product, compromises in the course of moviemaking are routine. Writers in Hollywood are notoriously unsung. Directors, with rare exceptions, have creative control.

> *The process of making a script into a movie is a little like making sausage— you really don't want to know what goes into it.*

"As a writer, you're a breeding dog," said Takashi. "When you have the puppy, they can take it and call it whatever they want." Still, without the script, they would have no story to tell, so Takashi did not feel completely unappreciated. He was reminded of his good fortune when he went to the film location for *Set It Off* during the shooting of a dramatic bank escape scene. A colleague turned to him and said, "All of this is happening because of something you pulled out of your typewriter." Heady stuff.

Though only half of Takashi's story made it onto the screen, the movie tapped into a deep vein among black audiences and attracted some notice outside the core demographic. The movie made a powerful statement. Black women especially could empathize with the characters who were young and struggling. The impetus for some of the story came from Takashi's observations of women he met while working as a legal services attorney. The authenticity of those experiences is what moved many to identify or sympathize with the characters. By that measure, *Set It Off* was a success, even in the writer's eyes. "I try to strike a universal chord," he explains, adding that the ability to make people feel for his creations is a reward in itself.

It helped that *Set It Off* became the fourth most profitable film at the box office in 1996: it cost $9 million to make and pulled in about $40 million in ticket sales. Not bad by any standard.

It is all about understanding the medium and the consumer, says Takashi. "You have to know your market," he emphasizes with the gravity of a man citing a cardinal rule, "because it is extremely competitive." And you have to be persistent, he adds. "You can not have talent, but you have to have tenacity."

The Uphill Climb

"I feel that I've had a lot of success," says Takashi, who is not only an accomplished writer but the proud father of a daughter, Kaaya, two. Still, some aspects of personal satisfaction remain elusive. "I haven't been able to cross over," he notes. "I've written race-neutral screenplays and met with no success." Takashi maintains that it will continue to be difficult for black writers, directors, and producers to offer a wider range of movie fare to crossover audiences until blacks vote with their ticket-buying power.

Movies that appeal to young blacks, such as *Menace 2 Society, Boyz in the 'Hood,* and *Belly,* are almost surefire moneymakers. The one black demographic that Hollywood can rely on is the twelve- to twenty-eight-year-olds, who will see a movie two, three, four times at the theater, thereby kicking up the box office numbers astronomically in comparison to the box office figures for *Beloved, Malcolm X, Rosewood,* or similar movies. No one, not even black audiences, are particularly drawn to those reality-based black experience movies that are frankly wrenching and difficult to watch. While the black community often complains about what Hollywood produces in the "black genre," we do not support "important" black movies at the box office and the violent, teen-directed films make a relative fortune, he says.

Takashi relates a story about having lunch with legendary actor-director Warren Beatty, who apparently sat down with every black person he could find while researching last year's critically acclaimed *Bulworth,* a movie about a white politician who loses his mind, starts telling the truth in rap lyrics on the campaign trail, and manages to fall in love with Halle Berry.

Beatty remarked at the time that *Devil in a Blue Dress,* the extraordinary Denzel Washington/Don Cheadle film noir based on a book by African American mystery writer Walter Moseley, was actually as good a movie as *Chinatown,* widely recognized as one of the best scripts and films of all time. But nobody saw *Devil.* The black moviegoing audience didn't support it and it flopped.

"When you don't go out and buy a ticket, you've made a statement," says Takashi. "We've had more variety than ever—*Get On the Bus* and *Rosewood* are two examples—but the people who criticize black movies that do get made don't go. The hip-hoppers do."

In Takashi's estimation, this young audience craves movies that provide political empowerment, strong characters who overcome their unfortunate lives by any means necessary. Story and plot matter less than whether the characters are smart and savvy and kick ass, a classic case of those without power gaining it vicariously for that two-hour period in a darkened theater. "That's the way it is," says Takashi. "Movies are consumer products and for black people they are political, social, and entertainment."

Bad movies that fit this bill get made all the time, while good black scripts with a different slant are passed over because Hollywood has less incentive to make more of them without

> *T*akashi urges aspiring scriptwriters to read, see movies, learn how stories unfold, and then start to write and do it every day.

some indication that they'll be profitable. There is an exception to the rule: Power is the great equalizer. Oprah Winfrey got support for the making of *Beloved* because she is Oprah Winfrey. She owns her own production company and her name by itself is a tremendous draw. But others who are less powerful, such as Takashi, have to justify any proposal they make with strong demographic indicators and market analysis before any project is blessed by the men in charge.

On the Marriage of Business and Art

TAKASHI learned the market not just by studying demographics and box office numbers but by critically analyzing what he calls "the anatomy of a film" and watching audience response. He is likely to go to see six movies in a row just to compare the dialogue, story structure, and director's style. His heroes are the usual suspects in filmmaking, Martin Scorcese and black director Carl Franklin, to name two, and he reads good writers— James Baldwin, Maya Angelou, Walter Moseley. Takashi urges aspiring scriptwriters to do the same: Read, see movies, learn how stories unfold, and then start to write and do it every day.

> "*The best thing about writing is that all you need is a pen and paper. There's never an excuse not to do it.*"

"The best thing about writing is that all you need is a pen and paper," says Takashi. "There's never an excuse not to do it."

The process of learning to write well is trial and error, writing and rewriting. "How did Shakespeare learn? How did Hemingway learn?" he asks. "Some of it is instinctive, but most writers just bust their ass. It's not easy to be good. You don't get to that point without really dedicating yourself."

Takashi Bufford knows he will get read and that producers, directors, and executives respect his work and appreciate the fact that he can draw an audience. But his major challenge is still frustration. Even though he is a successful writer and producer by any standard, real change in Hollywood is not coming fast enough for him. He uses his frustration as a tool, however. It motivates him to work harder and push for better and more black films. He is rarely stricken with writer's block and approaches writing like a puzzle, patiently fitting pieces together until the whole stands on its own.

> *The process of learning to write well is trial and error. Some of it is instinctive, but most writers just bust their ass. It's not easy to be good.*

As Takashi sees it, the television and film market for black programming will improve as studios and executives are forced to contend with the expanded need for product. "We're moving toward 500 [television] channels, and it takes 40,000 hours of programming to float a network," he says. "They have to compete." Since blacks watch more television than whites, networks will have to accommodate the demand, which will have a progressive impact on attitudes about diversity of programming and provide more opportunity for writers. In addition, more blacks are coming into positions of power and leadership, Oprah only one among them. Quincy Jones, another powerhouse, is rumored to be creating a high-end movie channel for black programming along the lines of HBO and Showtime.

Kid I Love It, etc.

AFTER his two years with the Disney program, Takashi was getting noticed. In 1993, he was hired to write the screenplay for the third in the *House Party* feature film series, starring Kid n' Play and, while writing the script, he formed his one-person writing empire, Kid, I Love It But You'll Never Get It Made, Not In This Town.

But Takashi believes he can do more than run a financially successful company. "We're at brick one of the empire," he says. "But things happen quickly in this town." While attitudes about race may change with glacial slowness, Takashi knows that his very next project could turn out to be the black breakthrough movie with enough selling power to overcome reticence about its profound subject. That takes a combination of skill and luck.

The skill he has—the rest he leaves up to fate. He is working on a number of promising projects, including an adaptation of a novel for a Lifetime movie about the National Basketball Association, as told from the wives' perspective; *Redgroove,* for the USA Network, about a campy black spy (à la Austin Powers) tracking a crooked cop through time; and another for UPN about a young black kid from Bedford-Stuyvesant who, discovered to be brilliant, goes to college and then to work for a think tank.

Any or all of these projects could take Kid I Love It . . . to the next level, or fail. But with Takashi's track record, it seems likely that success is the better bet—a sure bet if you consider his definition of success. "In this country, we define success solely in terms of money," says Takashi. "But I think you're successful if you're being paid to do what you would do for free."

CHAPTER 8

Changing the Way the World Thinks

Kent Matlock
Chairman and CEO
Matlock and Associates, Inc.
Atlanta, Georgia/New York City

Founded: 1986
1998 Revenues: $2.8 million
Number of Employees: 30
Initial Investment: $50,000
Current Net Worth: $4.5 million

WHEN ASKED WHY he chose the field of public relations and why he loves it so, Kent Matlock's forthright reply is: "Because you can be all-powerful. You can change the world."

An innovative and inspired media strategist and master of the persuasive sales pitch, Kent is the chairman and CEO of Matlock and Associates, an advertising and public relations firm with thirty employees and offices in both New York City and Atlanta, Georgia. Over the course of his career, Kent's clients have included Coca-Cola, Bell-South, Denny's restaurant chain, the *Atlanta Journal Constitution,* the Martin Luther King, Jr., Center, and Revlon.

Magnetic and articulate, Kent, thirty-nine, is proficient in the art of selling ideas, images and products. The craft and practice of spin have been much maligned in recent years, especially by politicians on the wrong end of a message.

Kent cites Coretta Scott King as one of his mentors, along with baseball great Hank Aaron and Hank's wife, Billye.

The best PR and advertising practitioners are considered arbiters of power because they have the capacity to educate and to persuade the world about what is important, worth thinking about, discussing, having. Good PR strategy makes public policy, wins and loses wars, decides elections.

In that light, PR and advertising take on more profound significance. And Kent Matlock is among the best.

Kent built Matlock and Associates into a million-dollar business from scratch, and his accomplishments are impressive. In the agency's sleekly stylish offices in Atlanta's Midtown Plaza near the world-renowned High Museum of Art, one wall is crowded with prestigious advertising and public relations awards. Among the gold, glass, and bronze statuary are pictures of Kent with various luminaries, including a newspaper photo of him sitting next to Coretta Scott King, listening with bowed head to something she's saying. He cites Mrs. King as one of his mentors, along with baseball great Hank Aaron and Hank's wife, Billye. Former NAACP president Benjamin Chavis and the King brothers, Martin and Dexter, are friends.

With guidance and allies like that, it seems success would be fairly well assured. But Kent earned every bit of what he has through hard work—and in spite of a hard head. He is the poster child for the saying that "experience is what you get when you don't get what you want." His

> *"Success comes from knowing where you want to go," says Kent. For him, that has always meant to the top.*

hard-won wisdom, business acumen, and creative talent have gained him the respect and favor of some of the biggest corporate clients in the business. Never one to fear jumping into the unknown feet first, he has done it with abandon, ready to swim for all he's worth.

"Success comes from knowing where you want to go," says Kent. For him, that has always meant to the top.

The Beginning

KENT Matlock was born in Chicago but grew up in Brownsville, Tennessee, a small town best known as the hometown of rock legend Tina Turner. He likes to describe himself as " a country boy," a self-deprecatory characterization that comes off as a little too facile from a man who looks like he stepped straight out of the pages of *GQ*. He is now a far cry from that kid growing up in a claustrophobically small town, working in the family restaurant and exploring a vague desire to write.

In high school, his sister's radio program piqued his interest in broadcast journalism as well as print. But in 1978, when he started college at Morehouse, the historically black men's college in Atlanta, he still had not figured out what he wanted to do with his life. Although he is from an old and distinguished family that includes judges, lawyers, an insurance company founder, and a number of successful entrepreneurs, he was torn. On the one hand, he had inherited a great and respectable legacy; on the other, Kent wanted to be respected on the street, to be a "bad nigger," in his parlance. Members of his family urged Kent to walk a different road, suggesting Morehouse as a start.

Morehouse gave Kent a sense of direction. "[It] made me understand that there were black men who had achieved great things," says Kent. "Things that changed the world."

A self-professed follower of the hook-or-crook method of skating through school, Kent was frightened by the academic rigor and the level of seriousness Morehouse men brought to their studies. "I was terrified when I found out there were brothers who were serious *and* brilliant," he says.

Pursuing his interest in the communications field, he found his way to the Morehouse public relations department. Dr. Hugh Gloster, Morehouse president at the time, and Dr. Alan May both a significant impact on Kent. Dr. May became Kent's first professional mentor. From Dr. May and others in the department (among the best in the field, according to Kent), he learned the basics of public relations and advertising. His professors brought the field to life for him while teaching him about the intricacies of media and how to write in a clear and assertive style. He learned the importance of the role of the spokesperson, how to judge what is news, how to attract media attention with events, and what to do with it once you have it.

> *The hand of fate slapped him upside the head. Hard. Life has a funny way of putting you where you're supposed to be.*

Kent describes Dr. May as a man who was able to teach how writing, thinking, and expression come together. It was exciting and energizing, but Kent, then immature and always searching for the fastest, easiest way, chafed at the confines of school. He longed for real-world experience and real-world rewards. He wanted money, status, and professional respect, and he wanted it yesterday.

Stepping Out

IN spite of the academic rigor Morehouse imposes on its students, in his freshman year, Kent took a job as a Budweiser promotional representative for black college students during the Kool Jazz Festival. He did a fabulous job promoting beer and even ventured to suggest that it might be a good idea for Budweiser to act as an independent sponsor of music events. (Three years later, Budweiser launched their Bud Superfest, a traveling music extravaganza.)

Never one to rest on his laurels, Kent took advantage of the reputation he was building to talk himself into a number of jobs way beyond his work experience. While still in school, he landed at a firm called Visual Persuasion and jumped soon thereafter to a position as an account executive at the Garrett, Lewis and Johnson advertising firm, which held the Budweiser account. In his work for Budweiser, Kent had impressed Ray Garrett as a smart and able nineteen-year-old who had a talent for persuasion—a little cocky maybe, but willing to learn.

Though Kent was Garrett's protégé, it could not make up for the fact that he was woefully inexperienced. Account executives are usually people with a record of successes and five or six years of experience in advertising and public relations. Kent was not even of legal drinking age, and very green. He managed to keep the game going for a while, however. Once on the job, he wrangled assignments on the Budweiser and Coca-Cola accounts *and* talked Morehouse into giving him credit for them.

Then the hand of fate slapped him upside the head. Hard.

"Life has a funny way of putting you where you're supposed to be," observes Kent. "At Garrett, Lewis and Johnson, I first heard the word 'nigger.'" He is not referring to the word itself, but to the first time it was directed at him as a racial epithet, a completely different experience from hearing it dropped in casual conversation. The former is the equivalent of standing at home plate and having the pitcher intentionally throw a fastball at your head.

"It was true that I didn't have the skills or experience to be a Garrett account exec," remembers Kent. "And this guy was complaining about it in a meeting and just said, '. . . and Ray has this nigger over here who don't know what he's doing.' Soon after that, the balloon deflated, and people would call me out about my naivete."

With the criticism spiraling out of control, Kent knew his days at Garrett were numbered. He delivered the work he had been assigned and started looking for other opportunities. He found one in 1981, in the guise of a man named Will Brown, a talented and creative advertising professional and one of the first successful black persons Kent had met in the field. "Bullshitter that I was, I convinced Will Brown to start our own business," says Kent. "I had a vision, but I didn't have a clue how to achieve it." Will had a studio in his house, and it seemed like the perfect setup. The combination of Will's experience and Kent's salesmanship fit well, but the business failed to take off. And Kent soon had other matters to worry about.

"By the spring of 1982, I'm cashed out, and my parents were coming to town for my graduation, but I wasn't close to getting my degree," he says. He had chased the fruits of success with such fervor that he had fallen way behind in school and needed twenty-one more credits (another year of classes) to get that piece of paper. His parents chalked up his failure to graduate to life. "My dad said, 'Those are the lessons you learn. You can do it.'"

Although Kent did not immediately give up working or the wine, women, and song that went with a nice paycheck, he did apply himself in school. He had to: He had run out of other options. His parents were tapped out, and he needed a job. "I didn't want to be a bad nigger anymore," says Kent, who stopped viewing money, pretty women, and a reputation as the sole measures of achievement.

He got a job—as a security guard at Pinkerton's, the detective agency that dates back to the Victorian era. "Pinkerton's deflated me," he admits, although the humbling experience was a good thing.

He took a more temperate approach to work and school, balancing the couple of freelance gigs he got through contacts (one project with IBM and one for Coca-Cola) with serious study. In May 1983, he graduated, and he did it with four years of work experience in his pocket. Free, he decided it was time for a change of scene.

Kent took $8,000 he had saved and gave it to his mother to make sure he'd have some money when he needed it—kind of a homemade insurance policy. Then he moved to advertising mecca New York City, where he again "got arrogant." Only finding a job was not going to be as easy as he'd thought. He spent May, June, and July of 1983 interviewing with advertising agencies without success. Then he got a call from Georgia-Pacific back in Atlanta. They were looking for a director of advertising and had gotten his name from Ray Garrett. Ray had retained faith in Kent's innate ability and was willing to recommend him now that he had more experience and a degree.

Back to the South

KENT took the job, which would involve public relations, advertising, direct marketing, and sales promotion. Corporate public relations involves a wide range of activities, all designed to build a positive image for the company, position it as a leader in its field, and call attention to the work or products of the company and separate it from its competitors.

At Georgia-Pacific, Kent took on those tasks and, in the process, sharpened his writing and editing skills, gained better perspective on how to improve product reviews and placements, and developed corporate and product positioning strategies for media, part of which was to create editorial and photo opportunities targeted at certain outlets.

Most in-house advertising people at large companies contract with outside advertising firms to enhance their in-house capacity. In Kent's case, that firm was world-renowned McCann Erickson, a connection that would come back to serve Kent well when he decided to strike out on his own.

While beefing up his professional capacities, Kent stayed in contact with friends he had made in the business along the way. And he tried a couple of ideas he had under his hat, the most notable of which was a sparkling grape soda he called Purple Rain. It was, after all, 1985, and Prince had just released the smash movie and soundtrack of the same name. What better way to push a soda than to have the world's most enigmatic entertainer put some muscle behind it? At least that was Kent's take at the time: that Purple Rain would be his ticket to independence. He had come to realize that he was better suited to calling the shots than running the plays, and he wanted to start his own business. At the time, Diet Coke was big and that provided the impetus for the new soft drink venture.

> *Even though Prince did not return his calls, Purple Rain (the soda) ignited Kent's entrepreneurial spirit.*

Even though Prince (who has since changed his name to the Artist Formerly Known as Prince, among other appellations) did not return his calls and Kent gave up on the idea, he had found new purpose. "Purple Rain [the soda] ignited the entrepreneurial spirit," says Kent, which was good, because he was restless and it was time to at least try his wings.

In May 1986, he resigned from Georgia-Pacific and started Matlock and Associates. He had maintained good relations with McCann Erickson, and they pitched him to McDonald's for consideration as one of their public relations/advertising specialists. Employing his smooth-talking talents again, he persuaded Atlanta's Midtown Plaza to give him a five-year lease, based on the promise of profits from the

McDonald's business. But he had overstepped once more. "It got right up to the wire and I lost the Mickey D's deal with a guarantee of $1 million in revenue by one vote. But I didn't hold onto the loss," he says philosophically.

In fact, the loss actually motivated him. He landed a contract here and there, building the business through his extensive network of friends and relying on savings to keep the company from flatlining. He called in his markers and looked to his mentors for support.

Slowly, he proved his mettle and constructed an impressive client list, first BellSouth, then Coca-Cola. He had gone to school with the King sons, Martin and Dexter, and created the new logo for the King Center. Mrs. King proved to be invaluable in helping to build his clientele, as did Billye Aaron, Hank's wife. The United Negro College Fund kept him on as a volunteer and paid him when they could. Sometimes Mrs. Aaron would give him money to make payroll.

Public relations is a word-of-mouth business. Satisfied clients and people with clout tell other potential clients. So it was with Matlock and Associates. Having established a reputation and a presence, the firm was ready when Denny's Restaurants came to call. Under fire for blatant racial discrimination against black patrons, including a group of Secret Service men assigned to the president's detail, Denny's pulled in a legion of PR people, Kent among them, to help rehabilitate its image. It was a chance to work with some of the best in the business—under pressure-cooker-like conditions. It was a testament to Kent's abilities that he was picked for the delicate job. Discrimination suits and other adversities (the Tylenol product tampering case is a good example) are a company's worst nightmare. Stock may rapidly lose its value under such circumstances, or the public loses complete faith in the product or service. Millions of dollars are often at stake. Image and perception are everything, and rebuilding both when panic sets in or high-profile embarrassments are recurring and undeniable is the ultimate test for a team of public relations specialists.

Kent agreed to join the Denny's effort only after he met with then-president Jerry Richardson (now owner of the Carolina Panthers), who so impressed Kent with his business sense and sincerity about ridding the restaurants of discriminatory practices that he became a close friend and mentor.

It was Kent's idea to bring a credible civil rights organization into the mix to convey that the restaurant chain was serious about not tolerating racism. As a result, Denny's joined with the NAACP in structuring the largest corporate agreement in history to increase minority-owned franchises. In 1994, Denny's paid almost $48 million to settle a discrimination lawsuit brought by black customers. As a further sign of its commitment to eliminate discrimination, every restaurant in the chain now displays a toll-free number for the U.S. Justice Department, so customers can call to report any incidents of bias. Finally, not long ago, Jim Adamson, the current president of the parent company, Advantica Restaurant Group, said quite publicly and clearly to Denny's 40,000 employees: "If you discriminate, I'm gonna fire you."

> *It was Kent's idea to bring a civil rights organization in to help convey that Denny's restaurants were serious about not tolerating racism.*

Under the PR team's direction, Denny's mounted an aggressive media campaign to emphasize its new pledge to diversity and tolerance. Since he believed in the sincerity of Denny's desire to change, Kent was thrilled with the success of the project, which not only bolstered his reputation but also went to the heart of his great aspiration to change false perceptions of and attitudes about race.

It is one of the reasons he started Matlock and Associates. "I wanted to build a business that changes the way the world looks at people of color," he says.

Of the impact of racism on his own life, Kent says, "Racism hurts you in one regard and helps you in another. I had managed crisis issues, I formulated great strategy, I had overcome things. So it helped me. But it gets you angry as hell." Apparently, that process is under way. In 1996, the Atlanta Business League, similar to a black Chamber of Commerce, recognized Kent as Entrepreneur of the Year.

A Young Veteran

AT thirty-nine, Kent has already been in the PR business for twenty years. Today, he is less self-centered and much more in touch with who he is and who he wants to be, he says. "I know men who have never wanted for money, but who wanted to be a great father and a good man." Those are Kent's goals, too. Divorced, with a three-year-old son, Kent says he has been a great father but wasn't such a great husband. "I wasn't a 'honey do' husband," he says. "I failed at marriage. I felt it infringed on my freedom. I avoid the things I don't do well, and it's hard for me to trust." Although he would like to fall in love and get married, he has no immediate plans in that regard. He does, however, plan to remain a great father. "Cutting the umbilical cord changed me. I feel privileged to have my son."

He feels equally privileged to have his family, especially after he lost his father to cancer in 1984. The following year, Kent moved his mother, sister, and brother from Tennessee to Atlanta. He is devoted to his family, with whom he is very close, and, surprisingly for a

> *"Search for the things that inspire you and have confidence there's a force working with you even if you can't see it."*

man who was such a hellion at one time, he goes to church every Sunday, no matter where in the world he is. "It makes me feel close to God," he says humbly.

He is also grateful to the city of Atlanta, which has long billed itself as the capital of the "New South." Kent emphasizes the need to give credit where it is due; in his view, Atlanta, particularly in the past twenty-five years, has fostered an open, welcoming environment that embraces and nurtures young black entrepreneurs. "Whether it is the legacy of men like Andrew Young and Maynard Young or it is 'the city too busy to hate,' Atlanta has fostered diversity and encouraged talent," says Kent.

To young would-be entrepreneurs who want to build a business in the rough-and-tumble world of advertising and PR, he counsels: "Search for the things that inspire and motivate you, believe in the things that can sustain you, have confidence there's a force working with you even if you can't see it. Plan your work and work your plan. Technology is becoming a great equalizer. There's no better time than now to do great things. Young people now have to believe anything is possible."

Information Systems for the Millennium

Neil Jones
President and CEO
M-Cubed Information Systems, Inc.
Rockville, Maryland

Founded: 1985
1998 Revenues: $20 million
Number of Employees: 110
Initial Investment: $300

E ACH CHRISTMAS WHEN Neil Jones was a child, he and his eight brothers and sisters would strike a bargain with their father. As the owner of a light manufacturing firm, Jones's father would sell his wares—cake pans, pots, graters, and other household tools—to his children at cost. The children in turn would sell the goods and keep the profits to buy toys. "I had no choice but to become an entrepreneur," says Neil. "I grew up in that environment."

Born and raised in a large middle-class family in Georgetown, Guyana, Neil pondered any number of career options, from professional soccer player to agricultural economist. Economics ran in the family, and agriculture was an important industry in post-colonial Guyana in the '70s. But when Neil came to America on a two-week visa, without money and with only the intent to study economics in college, his life took a detour that proves sometimes fate makes pretty good decisions on its own.

One of the prerequisites for an economics degree at Rutgers University in New Jersey was an introductory course in computer science, a field he had never heard of as a student at the prestigious, world-renowned Queen's College High School in the Caribbean nation of Guyana.

"I fell in love with computers, and that became my focus," says Neil, adding that he took the switch from economics to computer science in stride. It was the right thing to do. Neil, forty-two, is now the president and CEO of M-Cubed, Inc., a Rockville, Maryland–based systems integration company that helps clients solve problems by customizing business information technology systems to suit customer needs. M-Cubed, which is growing at a rate of 60 to 70 percent a year, does everything from buying the technology or software to building the applications and then making sure it all works smoothly.

How It Began

THE journey from indigent, immigrant student to systems technology mogul has been a uniquely interesting trip for Neil Jones, one fueled by a confidence bred into him from the time he was old enough to talk. He studied computer systems in the early '80s, long before "information superhighway" became a commonly used term, long before personal computers were considered a household appliance. An idea man whose mind is constantly working, Neil saw the need for technology customized to individual business needs way ahead of the curve and had the assurance to follow his instincts. It was a leap of faith. But Neil never considered the possibility of not succeeding at whatever entrepreneurial path he chose. It

> *When asked about his definition of failure, Neil responds, "I don't know what the hell that is!"*

was almost as if Neil looked the possibilities over and decided—as an act of will—that "failure" would just not happen. As a matter of fact, when asked about his definition of failure, Neil responds, "I don't know what the hell that is!"

Neil Jones is an entrepreneur's entrepreneur. A risk-taker, he is intrepid and thinks strategically and in terms of solutions, not problems. He gambles to win, learns from his mistakes, and is a winner-take-all kind of guy who fought long and hard and always knew he would rise, however frequently he fell.

Another Country, My Own

NEIL Jones's most indelible formative memories are his father's lessons about business and his years at Queen's College High School (QC). He talks about QC a great deal and clearly credits his education as the foundation of his business success.

"I would not be the person I am without Queen's College," says Neil. At age ten he was studying Latin, French, Spanish, and classic philosophy. At age thirteen and fourteen he was studying physics, chemistry, and Shakespeare. The Caribbean, like the rest of the Third

World in the '60s and '70s, was coming of age on a parallel trajectory with Neil.

"We were trying to find our way," says Neil. "Guyana got its independence in 1966. Those were formative years, and I remember them vividly. That's when my studies got more advanced, and I remember studying economics, microeconomic theory, and the development of underdevelopment. Everything was political, what you wore was political, what you listened to was political. What you read was political."

As Guyana shed itself of the vestiges of British colonialism, Neil shed his boyish innocence and internalized the lessons Queen's College taught. Once a segregated white school, QC followed the traditional British curriculum. Even after it integrated, the school catered to the middle and upper classes, instilling in its students that they were the future leaders of the world, invulnerable to failure and above menial experiences.

> *Everything was political. What you wore was political, what you listened to was political. What you read was political."*

By the time Neil graduated, his parents had divorced, and he had set his sights on America. His mother, he says, let her children make their own decisions, and he decided on the land of limitless potential. However, it was difficult to emigrate to America from the Third World in 1976, and the trip itself was a lesson in perseverance.

"There are restrictions on anyone coming into the United States. I had to lie to get out of the country, and there are a lot of other complicated factors. I got lost in Trinidad along the way [to the United States], and when I got to JFK airport in New York, the people that were supposed to meet me weren't there; we missed each other. I spent the night in the airport in Newark, New Jersey. I had a two-week visa, but I just needed a two-minute visa because I was never going back. I just needed to get into the country. I didn't have any money or family; I was the first Jones in the country."

It was September 1976, and Rutgers University in Livingston, New Jersey, was his only choice for college because he lacked enough information about the other 10,000 colleges in the United States to make comparisons. He learned more about the school through the West Indian grapevine. A number of students had left the Caribbean to move to New York and New Jersey. They attended Rutgers, so that's how he learned about the school and applied.

But Rutgers proved to be a good choice for other reasons. In 1976, the university housed the central computer system for the state of New Jersey, virtually a state-of-the-art computer laboratory for students. It was also one of the top ten schools in the country for the study of computer science.

He never thought twice about getting into Rutgers because he had graduated from Queen's, which, according to Neil, almost guarantees its graduates entrance to any school in the world. Neil Jones just had to figure out how to live. He got a job as a stock boy at Bamberger's, a New Jersey department store.

"I just needed a damn job," says Neil, the determination clear in his tone even now. "The interesting thing was I would never walk around the store with my stock boy's jacket on because I thought it was beneath me. I had challenges taking people's bags to their cars because I didn't want people to see me. People would give me tips and I wouldn't take them because Queen's College educated me for things higher than that, and it was unthinkable for me to do those things."

Neil Jones says he is not passing judgment on others, but he wants to make it clear that he does not believe in charity because he does not believe he ever needed it.

"I find value in [refusing to take tips] because I came here without a dime in my pocket," says Neil. "I refused to accept food stamps because it was demeaning."

Financial aid, however, did not fall into the "charity" category, and he "made himself eligible" for it. "I lied my ass off, but it [the aid] was a good investment," says Neil. "I paid off my loans and have employed a lot of Americans, so I have more than paid my debt back. That's why I can never run for office. Too many skeletons in my closet."

Neil may have scammed his way into the country, college, and a minimum wage job at a department store, but he was the genuine article when it came to school. Learning came easy to him; his challenge was to stay focused. He carried twenty credit hours per semester, a big academic load, in an attempt to get out of school before his immigration status caught up with him. (He became a citizen in the mid-1980s). He never took a communications or English class, which he saw as a waste of time. Instead, he honed in on economics and computer science with a concentration in artificial intelligence—which in simple terms means he was focused on trying to solve faster by computer any problem that a human can do. He figured computers were the growth sector of the future, even though he got some negative feedback from his peers, who wondered why he was doing all this "hard stuff and whatnot." He also faced more than a little skepticism from his advisors.

Neil refused to be deterred.

"I told the guys when I was in school, all those guys in communications, I said, 'You look for a job; you won't make a lot of money, even if you find a job.' I managed my career like I had managed everything else," recalls Neil. "I didn't trust my college counselors because to me they were people who couldn't get a job anywhere else. So when I got into the real world, I followed my own advice and shaped my own career."

He left Rutgers for a job and finished his degree later at the State University of New York external program, because the work opportunity was too good to pass up. He was recruited by Wilmington, Delaware–based Dupont in 1979, at the beginning of the technology revolution. Although the company could not promise a job in the field of artificial intelligence, it could promise something that would be technically challenging.

"I became a systems programmer, which was very unusual in itself," says Neil. Most systems programmers had five to six years' work experience, but Neil knew the IBM mainframe, which he had programmed on in the lab at Rutgers and which Dupont used. "Keep in mind this was the early '80s, and artificial intelligence was a gleam in most people's eye. You needed special equipment for it [in the '80s], and they [the computers] were multimillion dollar machines."

He began working as a systems programmer in December as part of a team that refined and maintained the operating system for Dupont's company-wide computer system. Neil helped develop a number of cutting-edge technologies along the way, including a system that allowed operators to manage mainframe systems remotely. This was ages before the modem.

And even though he was fascinated with the work and rarely bored—an important factor for someone like Neil, who has the attention span of a gnat—he was always plotting his rise.

"I remember at one of my performance reviews everything was fine, and my supervisor asked me where I saw myself in five to ten years," remembers Neil. "I said, 'Well, one guy is the supervisor (the man had been at Dupont twelve or fifteen years). He did it in twelve years; I'll do it in five. Seems reasonable to me. Then your job after that.'"

The supervisor, obviously surprised at the candid response, made the point that Neil was making good money at his current career level, but Neil wasn't going down that road.

"I said, 'Wait a second. My expectation is that if I'm going to be working at Dupont, I'm going to be running Dupont at some point in time,'" says Neil. "What was the difference between me and the other guy running Dupont at that time but experience? My point is that that was the philosophy I have always had. There's nothing I cannot do. You might have more experience than me, but that comes with time."

> *"What was the difference between me and the guy running Dupont but experience?"*

It almost seems that a man this confident would never have periods of doubt, but he does occasionally suffer the human weakness of professional insecurity. He grew up in a majority-black country, but the racial peculiarities of America are capable of affecting even those who did not come of age here.

"I spent the first few years of my career wondering, Did I get this job because I was black? One morning I said, 'I don't give a damn because I'm the best there is at what I do.'"

That settled, Neil looked hard at who rose through the ranks at Dupont, which taught him something about who had a shot at actually running the company and who apparently did not.

"If you look at who moves up in the company, there's a logic to it," states Neil. "At IBM if you want to be anything, you have to be in marketing. In Dupont's history, every CEO was an engineer."

He met with a manager other than his own for advice, and the man showed him his history at Dupont, basically how the political game at that particular company was played.

"You do work for somebody, you make him or her look good, and they get promoted. Once they get promoted," recounts Neil, "they drag you along. Now sometimes when they get promoted they can't drag you along immediately, but the first opportunity that pops up for an available spot, then they grab you. That's the way it is."

As goes life in the microcosm of the corporation, so it goes on the outside. Neil is reflective on this point and sees the story's larger relevance.

"That's the way most of life is," he says. "A lot of people we don't understand, and we call it the old boy's network, but that's the way things move. I personally believe that too many things are classified as racist or discriminatory too quickly. A lot of things are simply human nature."

Therefore he understood that Dupont pigeonholed him as a systems programmer for the six years he worked there because the company tended to think in those narrowly focused terms, and they believed he was too valuable an asset to lose to another technological sphere. When he wanted to advance his knowledge in relation to systems programming, the company made reasonable investments in broadening his skills. When he expressed interest in other aspects of the work—like learning the applications side of computing—the company was less than supportive.

Perhaps in an effort to demonstrate a good faith interest in his future with the company, Dupont recruited Neil for the Field Program, a management training program that grooms the best and brightest to be future leaders of the company.

In that program he met Tyrone Austin, a specialist in the corporate finance division who would eventually become his business partner.

Neil remembers that he rarely saw Ty in the context of the Field Program. But he ran into him at a mall in Wilmington one Saturday, and they began to talk. Ty told Neil he was planning to leave Dupont to start his own company, and Neil was intrigued. It was the beginning of several talk and planning sessions that would span the course of 1984 and culminate in the founding of M-Cubed.

Ty took a consulting job in New York and commuted daily from Wilmington to learn how a consulting business worked while Neil bided his time by getting his financial house in order. Neil refinanced his house to a fixed-rate mortgage and bought two cars, figuring that his credit might not be so hot after striking out on his own.

In early 1984, they started the business out of Neil's home with an original investment of

In the first year of business at M-Cubed, they made "nothing but a name for ourselves."

about $300. They incorporated in July of 1985 as M-Cubed, Inc., and Neil stayed at Dupont until December 1985. Then he found a job with extremely flexible hours as a tech support manager for the county of Newcastle, Delaware, and worked there for a year to build a list of contacts and make money while they got the business off the ground.

Neil remembers telling a neighbor that he was leaving Dupont at the height of the recession, and the neighbor remarked that he was crazy. Neil saw it another way.

"I saw security in my own capabilities," says Neil. "I figured if [M-Cubed] didn't work, I have great technical skills. I can go and get another job. Sometimes knowledge is overrated, and being naive is a strength that most people don't recognize."

In the first year of business at M-Cubed, they made "nothing but a name for ourselves."

> "*The future dictates. If you believe in the future, you gotta do whatever it takes to get there.*"

But in 1985, they made about $70,000, according to Neil, and got a long-term consulting contract with Dupont. It was just the two of them in the beginning, and it was a struggle to keep the business growing during a recession. Neil says that besides Dupont, most of their clients were small nonprofits that were struggling to pay bills themselves. M-Cubed started to hemorrhage money in 1989, and the owners made the decision to look for a more lucrative market than Wilmington. Neil struck out for the Washington, D.C., area and jokes that their second office was his briefcase.

Neil considers moving the base of operations from Delaware (where they still have an office) to Maryland a strategic sacrifice.

"We survived a recession after bleeding a lot in the '80s. Early on, with just a few customers paying the few pennies we were getting, it became clear that these customers were not going to get us to the future," says Neil. "That was an important learning curve. The future dictates. If you believe in the future, you gotta do whatever it takes to get there."

He traveled back and forth between Wilmington and the D.C. area, drumming up business, until they finally decided to share offices with a business acquaintance across the Potomac River in Rosslyn,

Virginia, in 1991. They moved to their current offices in Rockville, Maryland, in 1993.

Now the company has over 100 employees and has been on *Inc. Magazine's* 500 fastest-growing companies list for 1997 and 1998. Their clients include the U.S. Treasury, the Holocaust Museum, the State of Maryland, and IBM. Ty and Neil are both semi-retired from the business. Ty is the chairman of the board and Neil is the president and CEO, but the day-to-day operation of the company falls to chief operating officer Peter Jones.

Although M-Cubed is successful beyond most people's wildest dreams, Neil defines success as more than just professional satisfaction or wealth.

"Success must occur in multiple facets of your life. It's difficult to be successful unless you are paying some attention to your family, to re-energizing your mind, and to contributing to the community."

In the future, Neil would like to devote some time and energy to helping other entrepreneurs make their dreams come true. He is a self-avowed "strong Republican," a believer in the bedrock principles of a hand up and self-help.

"For me the future lies in creating some kind of venture focused on funding first-stage entrepreneurs and getting excited about their ideas." An interesting objective from a man who says he is not interested in legacies. "I'm really not," says Neil. "I think it is important for people of color to wake up. We spend too much time living in the past. If I can, through my actions, help folks wake up and take control of their lives, then that's good enough for me."

CHAPTER

Cleaning Up the World

Deborah M. Sawyer
President and CEO
Environmental Design International, Inc.
Hillside, Illinois

Founded: 1991
1998 Revenues: $6 million
Number of Employees: 47
Initial Investment: $40,000

WHAT IS A nice girl like Deborah Sawyer doing up to her knees in toxic waste? Answer: making money and saving the world.

Deborah M. Sawyer is president and CEO of Environmental Design International, Inc. (EDI), an environmental consulting firm specializing in environmental assessment, problem analysis, and toxic, hazardous, and solid waste removal and management. These specialty categories encompass a wide range of services, including air quality checks for asbestos or other airborne hazards and chemicals, cleaning contaminated soil, and removal and replacement of underground storage tanks to prevent groundwater contamination.

Incorporated in 1991 and now located in Hillside, Illinois, a suburb of Chicago, EDI employs a diversified staff of forty-five highly qualified architects, geologists, hydrogeologists, and engineering specialists, including civil, mechanical, and geotechnical engineers, along with two administrative personnel. Fifty percent of the staff are people of color and women—an unarguable refutation of the backward notion that minorities and women are technically challenged. The EDI talent has served a long list of august clients, such as United Airlines, Commonwealth Edison, Cook County, Kmart, Zenith, O'Hare International Airport, Citibank, and a slew of other Fortune 500 companies.

The company has grown from four employees and sales of $500,000 in its first year to revenues of $6 million in 1999. That is not surprising given that state and federal governments have gained some ground over the past two decades in the regulation of waste disposal, long an issue of contention between corporations and government. Increased efforts to tighten disposal restrictions on everything from hog waste to asbestos mean that waste management specialists, such as EDI, will have no shortage of prospective clients.

Going Against the Grain

ENVIRONMENTAL waste cleanup is an unusual career path for a woman, but even more so for a black woman. Deborah, forty-three, is used to navigating her own course. She turned down a full four-year scholarship to Johns Hopkins University to attend Atlanta's Emory University for, she says, all the wrong reasons: "It was sunny and beautiful."

Unfortunately, Emory counselors steered her toward the soft sciences (political science to be exact), despite the fact that she was a National Merit Finalist and had scored well over 700 (out of 800) on the math and science portion of her SATs. She reluctantly took their counsel but added a full pre-med curriculum. As a result, she received a bachelor's degree in political science and biology, followed by a master's degree in petroleum microbiology.

> "*We need to realize our own strengths and work toward our full potential despite what anyone else may do to try to dissuade us.*"

Deborah told *Black Entrepreneur* magazine that the lack of sensitivity to her strengths was characteristic and hardly an unanticipated obstacle. "Instructors need a certain amount of sensitivity training. They need to be aware of the subtle race and gender discrimination. If a student knows that you are only going to ask white males the math and science questions, why would I, being a black female, ever study these subjects?" asks Deborah, but she adds that each person is accountable to some degree for identifying and playing to their strengths. "We as individuals need to realize and recognize our own strengths and work toward utilizing those strengths to their full potential despite what anyone else may do or say to try to dissuade us."

Deborah Sawyer has received numerous business honors as an environmental entrepreneur, including the Woman Business Owner of the Year Award from the National Association of Women Business Owners, the Bank of America Small Business Award, and the Small Business Administration's National Minority Small Business Person of the Year Award.

But she started out like every other struggling entrepreneur, doing everything she could to make it work, from cleaning bathrooms to drawing a salary smaller than that of the first secretary she hired. In spite of her impeccable credentials, knowledge, skills, and experience (she helped write the Ohio Environmental Protection Agency's hazardous waste rules), her biggest challenge has been and likely always will be credibility, according to Deborah, even though she is fairly well known and has a platinum reputation in the business. There will always be the next client who has not heard of EDI and its dynamic owner.

Though EDI is federally registered as a female- and minority-owned business, an 8(a) company, which means that a fair amount of its contracts have been government mandated, Deborah has never relied on its minority/female status. That is fortunate because, in this era of attacks on all kinds of affirmative action programs, including set-asides, mandated contracts are fewer. It is no small impediment to have to prove yourself over and over again, but Deborah is a survivor and coolly sanguine about that reality. "You have to be able to walk the walk and talk the talk," she says. "You have to be able to back up every claim you make and know your business inside and out."

On that score, Deborah has no worries.

A Scientist in the Making

DEBORAH describes herself as a "mutant child," a rather harsh reflection of what life must have been like as a little black girl who was more interested in math and science than girls and black people are expected to be. Growing up in a comfortable, black, middle-class neighborhood in Columbus, Ohio, she was always experimenting and remembers mixing perfume with shampoo to determine whether she could come up with something better smelling than the ordinary stuff. "I would perform surgery on my sister's dolls, which usually resulted in a missing arm or leg," says Deborah. "But I wanted to see what was inside."

Fortunately, Deborah's family supported her inclinations. A clue to Deborah's strength rests with how her parents raised their children.

Her father died when she was twelve, but Deborah and her sister and brother had already absorbed the clear message from both parents that they were smart and beautiful and able to do anything they wanted, if only they followed their hearts and minds. "I had wonderfully nurturing parents who allowed us to do whatever we were interested in," she says, adding that early influences are what help her even to this day sustain her self-esteem. "If you don't have that when you're young, you might never get it."

Deborah retained her interest in science throughout junior high and high school. Seeking the best educational environment to foster it, her mother enrolled her at the private Columbus School for Girls. She was one of the few black students. Although Deborah believes that she received a first-class education, she was often treated like a second-class citizen. Once, Deborah was sent home because the grease in her hair offended the white girls. She was subject to those questions that many black people over the age of thirty-five who grew up in majority-white communities, will find familiar: Why is your hair like that? Can I touch it? Do you tan?

> *Deborah's nurturing and supportive upbringing helps her sustain her self-esteem today. "If you don't have that when you're young, you might never get it."*

By high school, she had developed a thick skin and important insight into racism. "Racism and sexism are a part of life," says Deborah. "And going to a school like that taught me white people are no better than I was. They weren't smarter or cleaner. I never had to be afraid of them. That laid the groundwork for all of my life. I can walk into any CEO's office and I am not intimidated."

After high school and Emory University, she explored the possibility of medical school but found her interest in medicine waning. This may have been largely due to her experience in the medical school interview process including one incident when one professor leaned over inches from her face and said with a leer, "You look like a girl who likes a good time."

Leaving the idea of medical school behind, she entered a master's degree program at Eastern New Mexico University, originally intent on a concentration in biology. She narrowed the focus to petroleum microbiology (the science of how to more efficiently use microorganisms to extract oil from its source) when she was nominated for a fellowship in the field. A professor actually picked her out of the crowd, suggesting that she might find the work fascinating. She did and won the fellowship, funded by a consortium of fuel companies. During her course and project work, which she describes simply as "using bugs to break down oil products in rocks," she managed a research laboratory dedicated to the study of alternative fuel sources and conducted some of the earliest research in the area of safer hazardous waste disposal.

Not really environmentally aware before her days in New Mexico, through this line of research she began to see the dangerous impact of toxins: "How many fish have cancer? How many birds are extinct because of the way we decide to store or get rid of this stuff?" She became an avid environmentalist and developed a fierce desire to clean up the world.

On the Love Canal

THE switch from political science to petroleum microbiology set her career course, and it proved to be a leap into the right field at the right time. Although the government began to recognize the need to segregate hazardous wastes from regular solid wastes in the 1960s, the issue did not come to public awareness until the discovery that toxic waste was being dumped at Love Canal, near Niagara Falls, New York.

In 1979, Love Canal residents were forced to evacuate their homes upon learning that hazardous waste leaking into their water supply from disposal containers was a threat to their health. Not only had they been exposed to a serious health risk, but their houses were uninhabitable and unsellable. Fueled by public outrage, the story was covered from coast to coast and around the world. The outrage and the attention the story received instigated a government investigation, which revealed that the Love Canal fiasco was not an aberration, that many similar sites existed across the country. That finding resulted in a wave of new state and federal regulations regarding the disposal of toxic and hazardous waste and the establishment of the Superfund, a federal program that allocates billions to clean up and control contamination.

It was during this first significant wave of environmental regulation and remediation that Deborah Sawyer landed her first postgraduate job. She was hired by the Ohio Environmental Protection Agency (EPA) as an environmental scientist responsible for writing the state's hazardous waste rules. As the person in charge of carving out the state's guidelines, she became a sort of diplomatic envoy between the scientists and the lawyers, two sides more akin to warring countries that speak different languages than colleagues. Not only was she able to act as a translator and to negotiate a détente of sorts, but she learned the two most critical aspects of environmental work: technical cleanup and the laws governing it.

Her dual expertise attracted any number of corporate suitors, and she was finally wooed away from the EPA by the Columbus-based URS Corporation, an environmental consulting firm. They doubled her salary and she developed their Midwest Hazardous and Solid Waste Management Group. At URS, Deborah worked long hours and often was teaching herself the job as she went along, but it was worth it. She significantly augmented her palette of skills, learning marketing, how to find and pitch clients, write proposals, and price jobs, and the finer points of field work.

> *Deborah became a diplomatic envoy between the scientists and the lawyers, two sides more akin to warring countries than colleagues.*

When Deborah's boss at URS was recruited to head up the Beling Company in Moline, Illinois, she went with him. Although she considers him something of a megalomaniac, she maintains that mentors can provide examples of what not to do as well as what to do. "People can be mentors as horrible or nice people, but [my boss] was a great teacher," she says. Deborah's mentor took her with him because she knew her stuff and she had built, from the ground up, a hazardous waste division that boasted $3 million in annual revenues.

Deborah was quickly approaching the top, and she finally bumped her head at Beling. After three years there, though she was a senior vice president, a member of the board of directors, and a division manager (none of which apparently stopped some people from asking her to get them coffee), she was effectively barred from company decision making because her boss ignored her advice. That was a problem, but the real issue was that she had reached the professional pinnacle at Beling; there was nowhere left to go. In case she hadn't noticed the bump on the head, she received an additional wake-up call.

Forced to Jump

BELING was struggling, and the bank standing by to infuse it with capital had a request: It asked that all of the company officers personally co-sign a multimillion-dollar loan to breathe life into a business rapidly approaching death. The president complied with the bank's request and boldly made the appeal to the officers. Co-signing the loan would make them jointly and severally liable. Deborah was flabbergasted. For one thing, every other member of the board was old and, honestly, she says, not in such good shape. It might sound cruel, but she said she had to ask herself: "Who's going to be alive and working in five years?"

In addition, her boss's general disregard of her input made her feel less inclined to take the risk. "He didn't mind me working myself to death," says Deborah, "but I wasn't really part of the decision-making process." She had to follow her own good counsel and refuse to sign for the loan. Knowing that her refusal would make remaining at Beling too uncomfortable, she thought about starting her own business, something that had not really occurred to her before. But she had in essence already done it twice, building divisions from nothing at URS and Beling, so why not?

"It was as much a surprise to me as anyone," she says about starting EDI. "But I thought if I was going to risk my money, I might as well risk it on my own company." She had $20,000 in capital gains from a house she sold in Ohio and her mother loaned her another $20,000. Deborah wrote a thorough business plan and started making the rounds to banks in January 1991. "Most of the bankers were white men and they didn't even ask me to sit down," Deborah recalls. "They talked to me like I was a stupid stepchild and here I had started two successful businesses."

She went to twenty-four banks before someone finally offered her a seat. The banker, a young white woman at the

> *The good old boy network is alive and dispensing favoritism, but women and minorities are breaking down barriers in technical fields anyway.*

Harris Bank in Chicago, listened to her story, considered her experience and credentials and extended her a $50,000 line of credit the same day. Environmental Design International, Inc., opened its doors in Glen Ellyn, Illinois, in March 1991. (The company moved to its current Hillside offices in January 1995.)

To this day, Deborah reports, her biggest issues remain fighting for credibility, respect, and financing. "As recently as 1994, an engineer at a large company said, 'I don't have to buy complex engineering projects from someone like you. I buy widgets and janitorial services from people like you.' He made me feel like I was going up to the big house to ask massa for another bucket of grits. It's like they don't believe I'm really black, really alive, and really in this business."

Her experiences make her philosophical about affirmative action programs, which she believes are absolutely necessary because they are often—in spite of ability and qualifications—the only way to wedge the door open a crack. The good old boy network is indeed alive, dispensing favoritism within its confines every day, but women and minorities are breaking down barriers in technical fields anyway. Deborah is happy to see this—she could use the company.

Although the first few years were rough, Deborah did not falter, even when she had to cash in a few IRAs once to make payroll. She did anything and everything she could to keep EDI alive, including working hundred-hour weeks. In 1993, while waiting for a reporter to come and interview her about the new business, she unexpectedly met the reporter in the restroom of the EDI offices. Deborah, in her work uniform of a tastefully tailored blazer, a skirt, and big yellow rubber gloves, was cleaning the sink. She matter-of-factly introduced herself to the reporter, shook hands, and finished cleaning before she led the woman to her office to talk. That was two years after EDI was founded and, although the business was turning a profit, Deborah preferred to put her money back into operations rather than invest in a cleaning service.

Helping Hands

IN the early years, EDI benefited from its certification under the Minority Business Enterprise program of the city of Chicago and Cook County. Deborah estimates that in the beginning, about sixty percent of her business came to her via affirmative action programs that mandated that larger firms contract some business out to minority businesses meeting federal requirements. But as her reputation grew, she depended less on that kind of start-up assistance and more on her reputation. Now, she can count on repeat business from satisfied clients as well as her excellent sales and marketing staff to boost business. Deborah's recommendation to other small companies, however, is that they get minority business certification, even if they are not interested in government contracts. "A lot of big corporations are now asking for certification so that they can document contracting with a minority firm to the federal government. It's become a routine part of their process," she says.

In addition to her mother, who is on the EDI board of directors, Deborah gives a lot of credit for her success to the Women's Business Development Center, a leading and aggressive advocate for women business owners in Chicago and nationwide. The Center has fought diligently to help create a positive economic climate for women-owned enterprises, and it provided priceless assistance to EDI. In that spirit of cooperation, Deborah now passes on her wisdom and knowledge by counseling and encouraging other women eager to branch out on their own.

> *A strong business plan is a must because if you are unable to articulate what you want to do and why and define your market, it isn't a business yet.*

A strong business plan is a must, says Deborah, because if you are unable to articulate what you want to do and why and define your market, it isn't a business yet. And, as she has learned, it is important to play to your strengths. "My major advice is know the stuff you're good at," she counsels. "And know at least two-thirds of your business, the technical side and the financials. You can hire someone to do the rest."

Like everyone, Deborah made a few mistakes at the outset. Her first, she claims, was to take on partners, whom she had to buy out when their vision of the business diverged. Second, in an effort to make EDI a comfortable work environment, Deborah recalls that she was sometimes "too much of a buddy and not enough of a boss." She has since created a delicate balance between discipline and freedom at EDI, but her get-tough stance helped the staff to understand that she was serious about the business and the work.

Sustained growth is on her agenda for the future, with plans to expand the services EDI offers, build the company into one that can compete for the billion-dollar contracts, and form alliances with businesses abroad. These objectives reflect a double bottom line: financial benefit for Deborah and her company and benefit to the communities in which EDI does its environmental improvement work. Deborah finds this work immensely rewarding because she is, in a real sense, saving a small piece of the world.

Calling the Shots

Sheila Brooks

President and CEO

SRB Productions, Inc.

Washington, D.C.

Founded: 1990

1998 Revenues: $950,000

Number of Employees: 7

Initial Investment: $15,000

Current Net Worth: $1.2 million

DURING HER THIRTEEN-YEAR career in journalism, Sheila Brooks earned a stellar reputation for her expertise in television and radio news, newspaper management, and prime-time television documentaries. That wide-ranging background came in handy when she started her own media company and, in the early years, did it all herself: writing proposals and scripts, editing tapes, hauling equipment, running cameras, and conducting on-camera interviews.

Now, as president and CEO of SRB Productions, Inc., Sheila has steered her company to the point where she can concentrate on expanding services, attracting new clients, and overseeing operations of the script-to-screen company (named for Sheila and her husband, Rodney Brooks). Though Sheila's talents and energies are focused on the big picture, she hasn't slowed down a bit.

Visitors to her spacious downtown Washington, D.C., offices are struck by the hum of organized frenzy. As her multicultural staff takes care of business, Sheila strides through like a general surveying her battlefield. With supermodel looks, a television anchor voice, and the dramatic flair of a leading lady, she fires off instructions and checks a million details a minute without mussing a hair or wrinkling her stylish power suit. The diva is clearly in charge.

Sheila and SRB are at the top of their game with an impressive client roster, glowing accolades, and revenues in the millions. Yet even as she oversees dozens of projects, she stays firmly in touch with two things: God and her roots.

Driven

AS a skinny, pigtailed girl growing up in a low-income neighborhood of Kansas City, Missouri, Sheila Dean Smith was driven to succeed. Her mother, Gussie Mae Smith, now eighty-two, worked two jobs to support Sheila and her sister, Pam. When Gussie was thirteen, she tired of picking cotton in Mississippi and moved to Missouri to work as a maid. Along the way she married, had her children, and divorced. Refusing to consider welfare, Gussie worked her way from maid to office cleaning woman to licensed practical nurse. She converted to Catholicism and sent her girls to Catholic schools to give them a strong academic and religious foundation.

"We grew up poor," Sheila says. Since they were bussed to school, "We didn't have friends in the neighborhood. With our uniforms, we were accused of thinking we were better than the other kids. And we got beat up a lot." All that adversity "made me a more determined, more independent person." Sheila recalls that she was a good student, "but rebellious," crediting some of her rebellion to the fact that she grew up in the '60s, at the height of the race riots in Kansas City. She remembers a brick flying through a window of her elementary school.

> *With supermodel looks, a television anchor voice, and the dramatic flair of a leading lady, diva Sheila is clearly in charge.*

Sheila's mother made sure the girls knew what was going on in their world and community by gathering them to watch the evening news. Five-year-old Sheila pictured herself as a reporter. Sheila's natural curiosity and interest in current events blossomed into a growing desire to report the news. She wrote a personal advice column for her high school newspaper under the name Mama Feelgood.

But she ran into roadblocks early. At Columbia College, a private, Catholic liberal arts college in Columbia, Missouri, she told her professors and fellow students of her plans to become a journalist. They suggested that she become a nurse or teacher instead. Blacks, and for that matter women, were a rarity in the hard news business during the mid- to late '70s, and there were virtually none of either in on-air positions of distinction. These were the days just before the gender and race revolution in journalism took place, right before people like Jessica Savitch and Max Robinson permanently broke the gender and color barriers.

Sheila, characteristically, did not let the discouragement of others block her path. "I thought, 'I'll write and show them!'" recalls Sheila.

One English professor saw Sheila's potential, however, and encouraged her to take writing classes. She took television production classes her freshman year and felt she had found her niche. She strengthened her writing with an advice column in the school paper. In her sophomore year at Columbia, she met and fell madly in love with fellow student Andre Detrick. In April of 1976, they married, and Sheila left school to be with her husband, who had decided to leave college for the navy. They were transferred often, from Orlando to Memphis, and finally landed in Seattle, Washington, in December 1977. She enrolled at the University of Washington to finish her degree in broadcast journalism.

The move to Seattle was a big plus for Sheila: There were numerous learning opportunities available for a kid looking to jump into the television news game. Like most young, inexperienced people about to graduate and searching for a way to break into the intensely competitive field of news, Sheila looked for anything she could find.

A Foot in the Door

THE search is always difficult for someone seeking a foothold. Lonely, a little bereft, and in need of professional advice and support, Sheila discovered the National Association of Black Journalists (NABJ), at the time a relatively new organization devoted to professional advancement of blacks in the news business. Wanting to meet others like herself, she immediately joined. As she neared her graduation date, Sheila contacted thirty-three television and radio stations asking about a job, and every one of them turned her down. She didn't know it at the time, but major-market television stations, like those in Seattle, commonly require an average of four to five years of writing, production, or on-camera reporting experience to be considered for a job. Sheila had none of the above. But fortunately, opportunity presented itself in the guise of Olivia Dorsey, a young black woman who was a producer at the local PBS station, KCTS-TV. Sheila asked Olivia for a paid internship.

"When I get one, I'll call you," Olivia promised. Dejected, Sheila gathered her things to leave. "Halfway out the door," she remembers, "I turned around and said, 'I'll volunteer.' And she had to hire me." That unpaid internship turned into a paid position with Olivia's monthly talk show, *Dial Line Nine.* Soon Sheila became a secretary and production assistant in the KCTS's documentary department. She also continued to work on *Dial Line Nine* because she wanted to see her name in the credits, "which reaffirmed my contributions to the production of the show."

> *Sheila was so ambitious that, while friends watched TV at her house, she would sit on the floor, a typewriter on her lap, and update her résumé.*

With her talents and drive evident to everyone at the station, Sheila moved quickly into a writer and producer slot as part of the station's minority training program. The show she worked on, *Stepping Out,* profiled such artists as Dizzy Gillespie, Lou Rawls, the Edwin Hawkins Singers, and Ernestine Anderson. Sheila stayed at KCTS for three years, working weekends as a news reporter at KYAC, Seattle's black radio station. In her free time, she wrote for *The Medium,* a black community newspaper.

Sheila was always on the lookout for new opportunities. Friends say she was so ambitious that, while they watched TV at her house, she would sit cross-legged on the floor, a manual typewriter on her lap, and update her résumé, "because you never know." With the help of her fellow NABJ members, she networked furiously.

While working at KCTS, she also began doing production work at KING-AM, a mainstream radio station, working with popular talk show host Karen Denard, who became Sheila's mentor. "Karen taught me everything she knows, pushed me to go behind the scenes and learn *every* job."

Up the Ladder

BUT the budding young journalist still faced roadblocks. In 1987, while Sheila was working at KCTS-TV and KING radio, the NBC affiliate station KING-TV invited her to compete with a Native American woman for a coveted slot in their minority training program. After they chose the other woman, KING-TV told Sheila she could wait for another slot to open or she could gain more news experience at KREM-TV, their sister station in the small, eastern Washington city of Spokane.

> *Spokane viewers called the station to compliment "that cute little colored girl on the news."*

She and Andre, who had left the navy several years earlier, packed up and headed to Spokane. Sheila was the city's first, and only, black female news reporter. It was a difficult move for Sheila, but it was hard for Andre too.

"The transition to Spokane was a tough one. He had trouble finding a job similar to what he had in Seattle," says Sheila. "However, he later landed a job as an engineer at the same television station I worked at."

Spokane viewers called the station to compliment "that cute little colored girl on the news," Sheila recalls with a husky laugh. She covered city hall and politics, became a news producer and weekend news anchor, and found her stock rising during the campaign and election of Spokane's first black mayor.

Sheila paid a new kind of dues when the station sent her to cover stories on white supremacists in the Aryan Nation territories of Idaho, where she saw posters saying, "Run, Nigger, Run!" The Kansas City homegirl kept her professional cool and reported the stories objectively.

Her dedication to her work was further demonstrated when she became pregnant and worked the entire nine months—literally, up to the last minute. She went into labor while delivering the 11 o'clock newscast.

A Roadblock

HER restless ambitions unquenched, Sheila moved her family first to College Station, Texas, for a job as news director and prime-time anchor for KAMU-TV, and then to Dallas for an executive management program at the *Dallas Morning News*. There, she worked in thirty-three departments, from the newsroom and accounting to human resources, circulation, and sales. Even though she excelled at every step, she was about to hit a brick wall.

"I finished the management training program in a record 18 months—most people took three years," says Sheila. "So I was encouraged to spend another eighteen months in a designated department working toward department head, which I would become when someone retired." It didn't happen that way.

When the time came to graduate from the program into a vice president slot as the white men who had completed the program did, Sheila found doors slamming in her face. This painful and humiliating experience only fueled her hunger to rise to the top.

There was no management job on the horizon, so Sheila negotiated a move to a television station owned by the Dallas Morning News.

Unfortunately, her marriage didn't fare as well as her career, and she and Andre separated in January 1988 and divorced in June. Worse, he ran up major debts, which, in the community property state of Texas, Sheila had to pay. She lost her sprawling suburban home, luxury car, and all her possessions. Friends rallied around with assistance and support, but her faith in love was sorely tested. However, her faith in a higher power and in herself remained strong.

The consummate networker, Sheila built a reputation as someone who knew where the journalism jobs were and knew the people to fill them. She helped several notable journalists build their careers. Her most heartfelt commitment, however, has always been to mentoring young people, whom she calls "my children," providing nonstop nurturing, career advice, internship and job opportunities, and introductions to folks who can help them along.

Success on All Fronts

SHEILA had become national secretary of NABJ and, on a business trip to Washington, D.C., in August 1988, she met Rodney Brooks, deputy managing editor of the "Money" section of *USA Today*. A second chance at love appeared much more quickly than Sheila could have imagined. She and Rodney became friends, dated for six months, and finally fell in love. When Rodney dropped to one knee to propose marriage, Sheila happily accepted.

"I moved to Washington, D.C., to marry Brooks, with a five-year-old son, $60,000 in debts, and a week's worth of clothes," she recalls.

But Sheila has never been cowed by adversity. She quickly found a job with Vanita Enterprises, a media company owned by friend and then-NABJ president, DeWayne Wickham. Sheila produced two weekly public affairs shows, which aired on Baltimore's WBAL-TV.

Working at Vanita gave Sheila a taste of the entrepreneurial life, but she longed to get into TV in the media capital of the world. So in 1989, Sheila accepted an offer to head the documentary unit at FOX WTTG-TV in D.C. With a staff of five, "I was at the height of my profession, number three in the newsroom, executive producer of the documentary unit," says Sheila. Her pet project, *The Color of Death,* a documentary that examined drug-related violent crime in racially polarized Washington, D.C., earned an Emmy nomination.

Sheila enrolled in graduate school at Howard University. While earning a master's in political science, she made her mark on their communications department, redesigning the advanced reporting course for seniors from a classroom setting to a full-scale working newsroom. She also redesigned the weekly program *Howard Newsvision* from a public affairs show to a newsmagazine format that aired on Howard-owned PBS station WHUR-TV. With Sheila as news director and executive producer, the show won several national programming awards. She did all this while running the documentary unit at WTTG.

Sheila felt she had found her professional niche, but when WTTG producers asked her to take over production of the new

morning newscast—in addition to running the documentary unit—
she said no. The extra responsibility involved close to around-the-
clock hours—but no extra pay. Sheila resigned and decided to go into
business for herself.

A Business of Her Own

SHE and Rodney had just bought their first home together, and Sheila
was nervous about not having a steady income, but Rodney encouraged
her and volunteered to contribute his business and financial expertise.
She developed a solid business plan and in June 1990, with a $15,000
loan from her husband, started SRB Productions, Inc., in a spare bed-
room of their house. Her strategy: to carve out a niche in top-quality
television video production and media consulting.

The plan was to produce
content for radio and television—
thirty- and sixty-second spots,
public service announcements,
documentaries, occasional news
stories for local affiliates and
networks. But it takes time to
establish a client base and to
find potential investors. "Starting a new business is, without a
doubt, the most difficult challenge I've ever faced," she says.

> "*Starting a new business
> is the most difficult chal-
> lenge I've ever faced. And
> when you're an African
> American and a woman,
> the challenges intensify.*"

"And when you're an African American and a woman, the challenges
intensify."

She gave it her all, but progress seemed elusive. SRB Productions
was considered for a number of national PBS programming grants
but didn't make the cut. Other firms promised contracts that didn't
come through. In the first year, though, she managed to pick up the
occasional contract here and there, including a gig to produce radio
spots for congressional and state senate campaigns and one to

produce marketing materials and public service announcements for the Maryland State Lottery.

Along with the support of her husband, son, and friends, Sheila called upon the bedrock of faith, in both God and herself, that her mother had instilled in her to continue with her dream. Buoyed by her vision of success and determined to make it big, Sheila showed the never-say-die attitude she got from her mom. "If I start something, I'm going to finish it, no matter what," she says. "I'm at my best when things are at their worst."

After what seemed like forever, Sheila landed her first big client, the AFL-CIO. She produced a video on civil rights for immigrants, which led to other labor-related videos for the organization's annual convention. Her work for the AFL-CIO secured the work for other labor organizations. As word of her sharp professionalism and high quality product spread, major companies began to seek her out. Sheila worked with a PBS station, cable stations, the United Negro College Fund, and Black Entertainment Television (BET). She also produced segments for the *Oprah Winfrey Show* and *America's Most Wanted.*

As the business grew, Sheila got on-the-job training in hiring and managing a staff, juggling clients, and staying on the cutting edge of new technology in the field, such as digital editing equipment. "Hiring and managing staff is quite different when working for yourself," says Sheila. "You need to hire employees who have passion for their work as journalists and TV producers *and* who also are comfortable working in a small business environment. The staffs are smaller, budgets are tighter, and there is always a frenzy of activity, always the pressure of working under a deadline, always the need to juggle several projects simultaneously." She learned, she says ruefully, not to hire friends, because small businesses aren't for everyone, particularly professionals accustomed to the comparative freedom of corporate budgets.

Forging ahead, she networked with mainstream professional organizations, seeking and winning new business. She learned to write winning proposals and made it a priority to earn the minority-business certifications that qualified her to bid for major federal government contracts. She invested hundreds of thousands of dollars in a state-of-the-art editing system and in a soundproof narration recording booth, which few production companies have in-house.

These changes allowed her to work for clients that include federal government agencies (the Small Business Administration and Departments of the Treasury, Transportation, and Housing and Urban Development), corporations (notably New York Life Insurance Company), and nonprofit organizations (the Leadership Conference on Civil Rights and the NAACP). In 1999, SRB reached a new milestone when it was awarded a three-year, multimillion-dollar contract with Bell Atlantic.

Success Is Sweet

TODAY, SRB is sitting pretty. The company—and its founder—have a dazzling list of awards and accolades, with folks standing in line for their services and bankers following Sheila around her office begging for her business. The girl who grew up poor and ridiculed, whom teachers steered away from journalism, is admittedly enjoying the fruits of success.

Sheila got two memorable presents on her forty-third birthday. First, she was named Entrepreneur of the Year by the Black Business and Professionals Network (BBPN), which honors businesswomen of color from the Washington, D.C./Baltimore area. Second, at a gala dinner, she was presented (along with screen stars Tyne Daly and Tippi Hedren) with the Woman of Vision Award by Women in Film and Video. Sheila says she was "shocked and thrilled" when, at the end of the evening, Tyne Daly led the black-tie crowd in singing "Happy Birthday" to her.

The awards continue to roll in. Not long after her birthday, Sheila received the National Association of Black Journalists President's Award, in recognition of both her professional accomplishments and her contributions to her colleagues and mentees.

Giving Back

RODNEY says he "never ceases to be amazed by Sheila's talent, achievements, and—most of all—her commitment to helping others." That may be Sheila's greatest joy, for no matter how busy she is, she always makes time to mentor young people. Hundreds of up-and-coming journalists she has met through her career and through NABJ credit her with their success. She also gives selflessly to the many community organizations to which she belongs, serving on the board of directors of at least five.

Throughout the whirlwind of activity, Sheila's primary focus is on God, family, and feeling connected to the community. She credits her faith with helping her learn to let go of the small stuff and keep her priorities in order.

"I ask God to do for me what I can't do. I've learned how to accept the outcome of situations and consider them to be the will of my Higher Power," she says. "I've learned that a setback is a setup for a comeback. As an entrepreneur, my burden is sometimes heavy, while other times the successes are overwhelming. I've learned how to balance the peaks and valleys," says Sheila, adding: "Oftentimes, with running a business and caring for my husband and my son, I have to keep faith in my principles; and then I achieve all my goals in the end."

As Sheila told a reporter who covered the NABJ awards ceremony, her greatest achievement is "having my son. Because I can instill the same values and principles in him that my mom taught me." They are the long-wearing values that may not be so visible upon first glance but have an infinite power to sustain.

"As a child I used to go around the house singing lyrics to a song that said, 'I'm going to be a wheel someday. I'm going to be somebody, I don't care what nobody says.' My mom taught us that we could do whatever we wanted in life. She gave us a sense of self-esteem and a true appreciation for education. By the same token, it is important to pass on to my son that the journey may be challenging, but there is nothing he can't accomplish."

Sheila Brooks is living proof of that.

A Good Call

Thomas Johnson
President
Wireless, Inc.
Boston, Massachusetts

Founded: 1994
1998 Revenues: $2 million
Number of Employees: 10
Initial Investment: $0
Current Net Worth: $3 million

THOMAS JOHNSON, THIRTY-FOUR, has gone boldly where few African American entrepreneurs have gone before. His brother David formally started Wireless, Inc., a communications consulting firm, in Boston in 1994 and was joined not long thereafter by brothers Thomas and Daniel and IBM colleague Tony Wray. They all became the guiding presence behind one of a handful of black-owned communications businesses in New England. Thomas has led in the development of a lucrative business-to-business enterprise helping corporations, government agencies, and their employees find the cellular, paging, and long-distance and local telephone services that best meet their needs. Wireless customizes service and product packages for clients, who get the added benefit of "one-stop shopping," and acts as an ever-present watchdog to ensure that clients are not being incorrectly billed for these services.

The pervasive, aggressive advertising for retail cellular telephones, pagers, and related services reflects the view in the business that individual consumers (exemplified by those annoying people yelling into a cell phone on the subway or in a restaurant) are the main users of these services. But Thomas and his partners had a larger, more sophisticated business vision.

Analysts have been predicting that the best business and career opportunities over the next twenty to thirty years will be in the high-tech telecommunications industry. What they overlooked is what Thomas and his partners saw: the potential business opportunity in consulting for corporations looking for ways to clarify the extensive menu of telecommunications services and technologies available and choose those best suited to their needs at reasonable prices.

Wireless acts as an agent for companies such as Cellular One and United States Cellular, customizing and packaging their products and services for sale directly to corporate and government clients. Access to corporate clients, including Genzyme Corporation, State Street Bank and Trust Company, the city of Boston, and Raytheon Company, also gives Wireless inside-track access to employees within the company. Thus they have found a way to exploit a virgin market and end-run the competition for the retail consumer in the process.

"We give the employees great deals, and we have a competitive advantage with respect to access," Thomas says. "They love it because it's been blessed by the corporation, and we're also meeting the telecommunications needs of their executives."

Creating the Niche

TO design the most effective telecommunications package for the company as well as monitor provided services, Wireless has devised a detailed evaluation function called CAMP, the Corporate Account Management Program. CAMP tracks and analyzes usage, value-to-cost ratio, and non-business-related use of corporate accounts and finds costs that are incorrectly billed to companies. CAMP also monitors inventory, guards against fraud, and provides customized invoices—a big benefit in a world where a basic residential telephone bill is nearly impossible to decipher. Corporations, according to Thomas, were losing money because the sheer

> *Wireless found a way to exploit a virgin market and end-run the competition for the retail consumer in the process.*

amount of information (on bills and invoices) is overwhelming and difficult to understand, as are the contracts with service providers. Telecommunications companies were able to profit in myriad ways from the confusion.

"Wireless is a telecommunications watchdog to make sure our clients and their users—corporations and their employees—are on the best plan," says Thomas.

It's a win-win situation. Instead of hiring in-house staff to track and handle communications services, companies can choose the cost-effective option of outsourcing to Wireless. Telecommunications companies, which have focused almost exclusively on the retail market, are happy for the entrée to the business-to-business market.

The company has been on an upward trajectory since David had his brainstorm. Wireless went from David working alone to bringing in $50,000 in his first year in business, to $1 million in sales in 1995, a year after Thomas came onboard. Now the company has ten employees and had $2 million in sales in 1998, evidence that Wireless has established a solid base of clients and is thriving.

> *"Telecommunications is the fastest-growing industry right now and African Americans have not really been educated about the field."*

Thomas Johnson believes in sharing the wealth. He maintains that there is plenty of room in the telecommunications industry for competition and plenty of money to be made. As an example of the sheer volume of revenue involved, the cell phone industry already had more than nine million subscribers in 1994 (a $12 billion jackpot); about fourteen percent of the four million people in the Boston area alone had cellular phone service.

Thomas encourages African Americans to look to the field for entrepreneurial or career opportunities. "Telecommunications is the fastest-growing industry right now, and African Americans have not really been educated about the field," he says.

A Fateful Call

WIRELESS was founded in 1989 by Thomas's brother David (the company was originally known as Mobile Communications and located in Woburn, Massachusetts) after he graduated from Boston College with a degree in economics. David was working part time at Fretters, a Boston-area appliance and home entertainment store, where he sold mobile phone services. David soon recognized the potential for a corporate market in these services and began consulting on the side to small and midsize businesses.

He called likely clients out of the blue, billing himself as a communications consultant who could analyze their long-distance and wireless phone services and demonstrate ways to save money on their phone bills. David offered to provide the service initially for free, and companies ate it up. The response from these businesses convinced David that he had struck gold with his idea, and he started to think about how to pitch the same services to large corporations. He found the answer in brother Thomas.

A math major who graduated from Duke University and holds an MBA from Case Western Reserve University in Cleveland, Ohio, Thomas had worked in marketing at IBM branch offices for eight years before settling in Cincinnati, where he got the call from his brother. Thomas had expertise in selling PCs to big companies, which gelled nicely with David's ambition to switch gears and focus on the corporate market.

David reports that he begged, promised the moon, said anything to get his brother to join him in Boston. Thomas, the oldest of three brothers and one sister, finally agreed, not only because he was intrigued at the opportunity his brother was offering, but because it was a chance to work and be with his family. David had also called their youngest brother, Daniel, and extended a similar request to him.

"It was a chance for us all to be together, and it sounded like a good idea," says Thomas, who is extremely close to his siblings. In 1994, he left IBM to join Wireless, which he and partners David, Daniel, and Tony Wray financed with their personal savings.

It was then up to Thomas to determine where Wireless could have the biggest impact in providing a service. They were doing well selling services to corporations for the first two years, but the business accelerated when the Telecommunications Act of 1996 deregulated the telecommunications industry and leveled the playing field for companies other than the Bell Telephone Companies to enter the market. The resulting chaos of competition placed a confusing number of options before companies. Thomas pointed Wireless in the direction of creating a way to streamline the selection process and translate what amounted to a foreign language for corporations that spend millions on communications capacity—much of it in unnecessary costs.

According to Thomas, there are a number of areas in telecommunications where many large organizations don't realize they are incurring extra expense. These include not understanding the details of the contracts they negotiate for wireless services and therefore paying for functions they don't use or for which they shouldn't be billed, such as hidden long-distance charges. Second, many users do not realize that charges for dropped cellular calls or bad connections are refundable or that in certain situations a pager is the more cost-beneficial option. Third, purchasing is often more prudent than leasing equipment. Finally, Wireless has found some companies use costly 1-800 (toll-free) numbers to market products in their local calling areas, a big and entirely unnecessary expense of which most are unaware.

Word of Mouth Is Good Business

WITH that level of thorough analysis, Wireless has made significant inroads with corporate clients and laid a base for future expansion. Thomas would like to be a one-stop shop for all manner of wireless services, a dream he and his partners have a good chance of achieving given their marketing savvy and shrewd positioning in the field. Clients love them, if the testimonials about Wireless are any indication of common feeling about their capacities.

"As you are aware," reads a letter to Wireless from Raytheon Electronic Systems, "we at Raytheon had major concerns regarding a change in the vendor providing cellular telephone service to our executives. . . . During the past six months, your organization, through its outstanding performance, has shown that there was no reason to be concerned. In fact, service has improved."

That is music to the ears of Thomas Johnson, who has established excellent customer service as the philosophy that drives the business.

Thomas and Wireless take client relations seriously, believing that their best advertising is word of mouth from satisfied customers. Wireless assigns an experienced account executive to each client, and that executive provides on-site delivery, product training, and technology briefings, among other personalized services.

"There is nothing more valuable than a client referral," Thomas says. Part of his promotional strategy for Wireless includes asking satisfied clients to recommend the company to other corporations. "If you're happy with my service, tell the world about us. Most small businesses don't do that, but it's thinking long term."

Thomas cites good service, mentoring, networking, and word-of-mouth recommendations as largely responsible for his company's steady growth.

> "*There is nothing more valuable than a client referral. . . . You can also never underestimate the value of chutzpah.*"

"You can also never underestimate the value of chutzpah," he adds.

Two years ago, he met Frank Palmara, the former COO of the New York Stock Exchange, who happened to be having problems with his personal pager. Palmara had asked his daughter, Bobbi, who uses Wireless's services, where he could find a pager that worked. After she waxed rhapsodic about Wireless, he bought a pager through the company and casually said to Thomas, "If there's anything I can do for you, let me know."

That's all Thomas needed. He soon called Frank back, told him the Wireless story, and said that they could always use an advisor of his caliber. To Thomas's surprise, Frank was impressed enough to fly to Boston to talk with the Wireless team. The meeting resulted in Frank agreeing to advise them on the business. "He said he liked us and he liked our energy and, frankly, he was interested in helping us because we were a small black company without access to his level of expertise. He wanted to give us that," reports Thomas, who appreciates Frank's understanding of the obstacles they face as an African American company.

"Racism can preclude access," he admits, although he tries not to automatically jump to that conclusion when barriers arise. While racism is a fact of life for minority businesses, human nature dictates that people do business with other people who look like them, he says.

> *"Being a person of color and overcoming obstacles all your life means you're conditioned to overcome."*

What that means for Wireless is the same old story: They have to work harder and smarter. "We have to figure out every day how to be more competitive," says Thomas. "But being a person of color and overcoming obstacles all your life means you're conditioned to overcome."

Having a mentor like Palmara definitely helps. "He's like a father to me. I can call him up when I have a problem, and he helps me out," says Thomas. The relationship also gives him entrée to new relationships with potential corporate clients. "When I talk to companies, I tell them about my relationship with Frank," he states. "[It] helps to establish credibility with potential clients because he is helping us run our business more effectively." Thomas also makes a point of encouraging companies with whom he comes in contact to follow suit and mentor other minority businesses who may not have access to high-powered expertise.

Giving Back

THE health and well-being of other minority businesses is high on Thomas's list of concerns, as is his personal commitment to giving back on a personal level, something he attributes to his family and economic background.

He grew up in a low-income, single-parent household in his native Oberlin, Ohio. His parents divorced when he was six. His mother worked in a factory, and his father was a plumber. They pushed all their children to perform in school, rewarding them with a dollar for every "A" they received on school report cards. But their parents also set an example in everyday life. His father taught Thomas, "If you do good, good will come to you." It was not unusual for his dad to fix an old lady's burst pipes for free if she could not afford the service call.

His mother had eight children; Thomas is the oldest of the second set of four. School offered him a haven from the chaos at home, and he loved learning and the strokes he received for being a top student, although he did not think much about college. It was his father who pushed him on to higher education, for which he is eternally grateful. His mother is now a Catholic nun, and Thomas has a close, happy relationship with both parents, as well as dedication to the principles he gleaned from their teachings.

Although he is tremendously proud of Wireless and wants to build the business, he is less motivated by money than he is by the desire to build a legacy. Not only is Thomas Johnson community-minded, but he has seen to it that his company is as well. He describes Wireless as a "socially conscientious company," which contributes a portion of its profits to communities and charities through the Commitment to the Community program. And the business is actively involved in the community in other unique ways. As part of the Phone Alert Nine-1-1 Emergency Calls (PANEC) program, a joint effort by Wireless

> *Wireless is a "socially conscientious company," which contributes a portion of its profits to communities and charities.*

and the Boston Police Department, Wireless donated 100 cell phones as well as monthly access and air-time charges for a year to women who were high-risk victims of domestic violence.

The two programs are a natural outgrowth of Thomas's philosophy about giving and sharing. Not only is he a mentor for young people, but he has informally adopted two young at-risk men he met through a church program in Atlanta in 1992. Dontae Loundy, seventeen, and Darryl Stone, nineteen, have found a stable presence in Thomas, who gives them the love and support they could not find at home. When he first met them, they were disillusioned, ignored by the educational system, and wary of getting too close to anyone for fear of abandonment. But Thomas has been there all along and has patiently fostered their sense of self-worth by believing that they can achieve, that they are young men worth his time and attention. Under his tutelage, he says, they have blossomed. He is teaching Darryl the business, and Dontae has become an A student.

As for the company, it will continue to aggressively market its services and seek out new opportunities in the rapidly changing telecommunications field. In 1998, Thomas bought out David in a "friendly takeover." David moved on to found America's Choice, a telecommunications reseller focused on the retail market, and Daniel created Cellular Associates, which buys telephones and other equipment from corporations going out of business for wholesale resale. As cable companies and other industries vie furiously for the right to expand to the telecommunications field, Thomas, Wireless, and the Johnson brothers can sit back and plot the rise of a family empire.

CHAPTER

13

Designing Man

Stephen Alves

President and CEO

Alves Contracting Company, Ltd.

Washington, D.C.

Founded: 1983

1998 Revenues: $800,000

Number of Employees: 5, plus variable number of contract workers

Initial Investment: $0

Current Net Worth: $1.2 million

STEPHEN ALVES, THIRTY-FOUR, is a visual, tactile being. A lover of symmetry and line, color and texture, he has appreciated the look and feel of beautiful rooms for as long as he can remember. The sole owner of Alves Contracting Company, he is accomplished in the arts of building, design, and renovation. Much more the aesthete than is needed for basic construction work, Stephen is an artist at heart who endures the residential and commercial construction side of the business as a means to an end. What he really looks forward to is completing the infrastructure so that he can indulge his creative vision.

"I hate construction, but I love design," says Stephen, who, at over six feet tall with a linebacker's build, is not the stereotypical image of the sensitive artist. "Construction for me means framing the design. I love walking into an empty space and laying it out. Some people can't do that, but I have the capacity to see the finished product."

Stephen also has mastered basic building skills, which means that he is good at doing nearly everything he would prefer not to focus on—plastering (a dying art in the age of drywall), painting, frame construction, masonry, tiling—all of which he patiently endures as he looks forward to the fun part. He is an architectural devotee who can find something to love in almost any style of building, appreciating the individuality of the structure, the way it meets the needs for its intended use, and its solid, technical soundness. But it is the aesthetics that satisfy his soul, particularly if the building is an original creation or was a hulking, empty shell he has brought back to life.

In 1983, between graduating from high school and entering historically black Howard University to major in political science and business, Stephen Alves formed what eventually became a full-scale contracting company specializing in commercial and residential construction, renovation, and restoration. He founded Alves Contracting Company at the age of seventeen while working part-time as a front-desk clerk at a residential building in downtown Washington, D.C. What began with a series of commercial cleaning contracts (Stephen describes himself as an obsessive-compulsive cleaner) evolved slowly into an enterprise that helps home and property owners design and build the space of their dreams.

Over the past seventeen years, the business has grown and changed on a parallel track with Stephen's personal development, experience, and discovery of what he really enjoys, where he wants to concentrate his time and energy. Now, Alves Contracting Company has a core of five employees who are multi-skilled, master craftsmen and is expected to bring in between one and two million dollars in revenue in 1999. Stephen is in the process of subcontracting more of the cleaning and basic construction work so that he can concentrate on renovation, restoration, and design. To free him even more for this aspect of the business, he is searching for a business partner who can focus on the numbers.

> *"Construction for me means framing the design. I love walking into an empty space and laying it out."*

The future of the business, like its past, will likely be fluid. Stephen has not decided where he ultimately wants to go with it. He is in the wide-open thinking and planning stages but, for now, renovation, restoration, and design are the emphasis.

Where It All Started

STEPHEN'S fascination with design and, by default, building is traceable to an uncle who owned a heavy commercial construction company in his native Trinidad. From the time he was four, Stephen hung out at his uncle's business, watching and listening as his uncle explained and demonstrated its workings to his children and nephews. Perhaps it really began at the age of six, when his aunt would hire him to clean her house. He paid a lot of attention to detail—pulling out drawers, wiping out crevices, and cleaning the places no one else ever looked. While cleaning, he also studied how things fit: how colors and styles complemented or detracted from one another, the consistency and grace of lines, the heavy solidity of well-constructed pieces.

Just before Stephen entered second grade, his family emigrated from Port of Spain to Washington, D.C. When they first arrived, Stephen often sat up at night listening to the neighbors talk outside his window because he thought they sounded so strange. Throughout this period of adjustment to a new culture, he "redecorated" the house repeatedly while his mom was out. "My mother would go to work and come home and I would have re-arranged the whole house," says Stephen, laughing. "I knew I loved style."

> "*W*hen I got to St. Anthony's High School, I had already painted it. I charged $25 a class-room." Stephen was four-teen at the time.

He was a responsible kid from the start, serious about seeking cleaning, painting, or light construction jobs, and always interested in learning some new aspect of the building and design trades. A tradesman named Mr. Datcher, who was getting too old to do work on his own, hired the ten-year-old Stephen and taught him to paint. Stephen considered it a learning experience, not just an opportunity to make some spending cash—although the money was a lovely side benefit.

His learning sessions with his uncle and Mr. Datcher set a precedent for the way Stephen learned his various crafts, picking up skills along the way by trial and error, by painstakingly recreating from scratch work he observed others doing, by figuring it out on his own. He was so earnest about setting a schedule and finishing a job on time while doing carefully precise work that people hired him for jobs requiring greater skill and responsibility based on their satisfaction with his completion of simpler tasks.

As a result, throughout childhood and adolescence, he was always working, honing and widening his growing spectrum of skills. By the time he entered high school, he was doing professional-level work. "When I got to St. Anthony's High School, I had already painted it," says Stephen. He had struck up a conversation with the priest/principal of the Catholic school and so impressed him that the priest offered Stephen the entire painting job. Stephen was fourteen at the time. "I charged $25 a classroom," he recalls.

Seizing an Opportunity

WHEN he was seventeen, all the odd and summer jobs, informal training, and experience culminated in the cleaning business that Stephen started after a bank foreclosed on the developer of the condominium building where he worked. A realtor took over management of the building and unsold units, the old cleaning company was fired, and Stephen offered to step in as a temporary replacement.

First he was limited to cleaning, but the real estate company was so satisfied with the work that when Stephen suggested doing some light renovation on the units, they readily agreed. He got a friend from high school to help, cut his uncle's logo off an old business card, attached it to one bearing his company name, and what had been a series of odd jobs became Alves Contracting.

"We plastered, painted, refinished bathtubs, replaced light fixtures, and cleaned the carpets," says Stephen. "We pulled twenty-four-hour shifts and were paid $1,200 to $1,700 per unit. It cost very little to renovate (in terms of materials), so we made about a fifty percent profit."

Word about him and the quality of his work spread in the commercial real estate community. Soon he was engaged to do renovation, cleaning, and some on-site management at apartments in nearby northern Virginia and landed some large cleaning contracts with the Association of American Publishers, the Hungarian Reformed Federation of America, and Thomas Pheasant, Inc., one of the most prestigious upmarket interior design firms in Washington. When he met Thomas Pheasant at his home, Stephen says, he was blown away. "It was awesome," says Stephen. "The moldings were consistent with the house, the floors were consistent. Instead of butchering the house, making it over into something it was never intended to be, the renovators had looked at the character of the house and restored it in a way that fit the structure."

Stephen realized then that he wanted to do the same thing: restore a house to its original glory, down to the meticulous detail. He loved the idea of bringing something back to life, but it was a practical notion as well. He didn't think he would ever be able to afford such a house for himself otherwise.

Washington is a contractor's dream. It is full of renovated and carefully restored nineteenth- and early twentieth-century residences, and the prices reflect the work that has gone into them. In some neighborhoods, these homes range from $300,000 to over $1 million. Stephen developed a close relationship with Pheasant and through him was introduced to the world of million-dollar renovations/restorations. It opened up new vistas of possibility for Stephen, who dreamed of bringing the same quality of work and vision based on architectural integrity to a wider market, although on a smaller scale. Specifically, he wanted to be a resource for the upper-middle-class African American community, offering consulting services as well as access to high-quality custom restoration and renovation work.

> *Stephen dropped out of Howard. "I kept thinking, Why am I here when I already make more money than the professors?"*

Energized, Stephen made a promise to himself to take Alves Contracting in that direction, but at present he was swamped with work, doing a briskly profitable business cleaning, handling property management, and overseeing subcontracted crews working basic construction. He had dropped out of Howard, a decision that he often questions now, but at the time it made perfect sense. "I kept thinking, Why am I here when I already make more money than the professors?" He got married and imagined a future doing large-scale renovations. It would be something to work toward, to look forward to, he thought. But fate intervened.

Renovating the Hard Way

WHILE living elsewhere, he bought a historic fixer-upper on Delafield Place in Washington, took out a loan for $25,000, a more than adequate sum for the work needed, and hired a contractor. With most of his attention diverted to his own business, the job on Delafield became a nightmare. The contractor ran through all of the money before a third of the work was finished.

"I had to do it myself," says Stephen, which meant that he was working virtually around the clock, managing the contracting business and finishing his house at night. It was extremely difficult, but with the help of a carpenter referred to him, he was able to complete the house where his family would live. He had already learned by happenstance what he could not do. "I don't do plumbing," says Stephen. "I once flooded a $400,000 house and I figured I would stay away from that." But he did the plastering, tiling, painting, and carpentry. When he finished it was beautiful. "The Delafield house gave me a lot of confidence," he says, and it added to his reputation. "That led to a lot of other restoration jobs."

Stephen went on to renovate and restore the lobbies and halls of thirteen low-rise Virginia condominiums where unit sales had been desultory at best. When he finished, people were clamoring for them, but, while the final product made him proud, the work experience was not a pleasant one. Someone was constantly calling the Virginia state building inspector to check the site, building permits, and the quality and progress of the work, which ironically was slowed by all the state interference, the double- and triple-checking of documentation.

> *Stephen came from Trinidad, from a culture where black folks are the norm, not the exception, and there is nothing even remotely equivalent to American racism.*

Stephen would complain good-naturedly about the constant interruptions to the property manager, George Ellis, with whom he had a friendly working relationship. Finally, George took pity on Stephen and explained it to him. "You don't understand," Stephen recalls George saying. "You're a big black guy and [they think] you're robbing them blind."

Stephen had no idea what George was talking about. Although he had lived in the United States for about eighteen years by then, he had been socialized in Trinidad, in a culture where black folks are the norm, not the exception, and there is nothing even remotely equivalent to American racism.

After Ellis said it for the third time, Stephen finally made the connection and it was like the scene from the classic black satire *The Watermelon Man,* in which a white bigot becomes black overnight. "The white guy looks in the mirror and he realizes he's black and he screams. I never questioned myself before that time. If I got in trouble, it was because I was Stephen Alves, not Stephen Alves, the big black guy."

Just as he was making advancements in the field of renovation and restoration, his psyche took this sudden, crippling blow. "I wasn't as self-confident after that," he laments. "And it may have had a financial impact because I was more cautious about entering certain situations."

FIGURE 13.1.
*The Mount Pleasant Victorian
shell waiting for Stephen's magic.*

Although his world outlook was permanently altered, George
Ellis offered him more work, and his faith helped Stephen make peace
with the reality of racism. The Delafield project went a long way toward reassuring him that he was good at what he did, as did the calls
from potential clients who had seen his work and wanted him to
work with them. And while the business took off in its new direction,
he again found a property he wanted to reclaim, an opportunity to
put effort and sweat into something personal.

Located in the historic Mount Pleasant district in northwest
Washington, the house was a run-down, uninhabitable Victorian shell
without a roof. He bought it for a song and began the long process of
restoring and renovating the house himself from the ground up. The
long road from conception to completion of the brownstone Victorian
took six months. But it was worth it. When he finished, he had created
a showplace with ten-foot-high ceilings, creamy plaster walls, hardwood floors, and chest-high wainscoting in rooms that flowed into one
another with grace and ease. The house was such a success that it

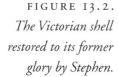

FIGURE 13.2.
*The Victorian shell
restored to its former
glory by Stephen.*

became and still is the advertisement for Alves Contracting, as a full-color photo in the local Yellow Pages. The success of the project also brought in a number of loyal clients, including the U.S. Naval Academy, Nationwide Insurance, and the president of the World Bank.

While Stephen has full faith in his ability to do excellent work—a faith that is reinforced daily and evidenced by the fact that he cannot accept all the work requests he receives—he has little patience for the financial management of the business. An artisan first and a businessman by necessity, he is searching now for a way to make peace with the parts of entrepreneurial life he does not relish.

Over much of the past seventeen years, Stephen has done more basic residential and commercial construction work than he would have liked, putting his dream of large-scale, historic renovation/restoration work on hold. He has been able to do some design and renovation for upper-middle-class African Americans but, again, not as often as he would wish. He has tended to drift where available work took him rather than focus has on what he prefers to do. That he has taken steps to change. As his reputation has grown, he has been able to choose the jobs and clients he wants, which means more planning, design, and residential restoration and renovation.

Now and the Future

WHILE Stephen Alves has been able to realize his ambition of bringing high-quality artistry and design work to a market rich with good-economy extra cash and a desire for custom restoration and renovation, he has had to grapple often with staffing and financial issues and has had problems finding people with the level of expertise he requires for his projects and whose pride in their work matches his own. On top of that, Stephen expects his workers to put in long hours when necessary. It is easy to find people with some of the characteristics he is looking for, but finding a worker who meets all the criteria has been more hit or miss than he likes to think about.

An artisan first and a businessman by necessity, Stephen is searching for a way to make peace with the parts of entrepreneurial life he does not relish.

Constant vigilance wears his patience thin and it's not really his style to kick butt, even when it's warranted. "I used to be a hard-ass and I found it was bad for morale," he says about his internal staffing difficulties. "I had to find people whose personalities are consistent with mine, who are self-starters." Over the years, Stephen has managed to do just that and now has a small coterie of loyal craftsmen (carpenters, plasterers, plumbers, and masons) who share his philosophy and approach to their craft.

Along with the worker concerns are client issues, such as people who believe that adding extras to the contract here and there should not cost any more although it of course adds time and materials to the project. "There are problems with people understanding costs, and I'm part of the problem because of what I want to deliver," says Stephen, who is such a stickler for fulfilling his own expectations that he often finds it difficult to cut back on the quality of materials and refuses to take cost-saving measures he feels may cheapen the final product. There is also the issue of not understanding how far a dollar actually goes in the process. "People typically want more than they're willing to pay for," he notes.

Making peace between his vision, high standards, and what people can afford is a tough balancing act because Stephen tends to empathize and commiserate with his clients. If he had to name the mistakes he has made in business, beyond money management, it would be not keeping a professional distance. "I'm too friendly with my customers. Often I need to step back and get some perspective."

> *Stephen's advice: Apprentice yourself, maintain control over whatever you do, and start with strong accounting.*

When asked what advice he has for someone who wants to enter the field, he is quick to answer: "Maintain control over whatever you do. And you have to apprentice. Construction is a second-generation business. You learn it best if someone hands their skills down to you." After a beat he adds, "And start with strong accounting."

Money matters, such as collecting outstanding debts and negotiating a price that is reasonable and fair for him, plague Stephen. Since he is usually willing to give more and absorb the extra cost, he admits he must be more hard-line in his bargaining for the financial sake of the business.

But growth is not an issue, as he sees it. "The business grows as fast as I want it to," he notes, pointing out that he has taken Alves Contracting from cleaning and property management to commercial renovation to residential restoration without much disruption during those fairly diverse transitions. A steady cash flow associated with long-term cleaning and property management contracts now makes it easier to get banks to extend credit to the business. Renovation and restoration are projects rather than long-term relationships, which means the money is less predictable although there is more of it. So now that the company has shifted its emphasis in the type of work it is doing, it is important for Stephen to find a business manager who can put revenue and payout management at the heart of their work.

Nevertheless, the company is turning a profit. Indeed, the business was self-financed until 1996, when Stephen took out his first loan, and most of the money he makes goes back into the business. "I reinvest primarily in equipment, tools, and people," says Stephen, adding with a laugh, "Except when I go to Neiman Marcus, but that's therapy."

Stephen Alves is flexible about what's on the horizon, but whatever he does it will be creative. He has a desire to pursue more artistic endeavors such as painting and he is leaving the door open for opportunity. With the economy booming, people are spending money to renovate and restore their houses, so there is more work available than good contractors to meet the demand. Right now, Stephen has the luxury of turning down work and has been picking and choosing jobs, envisioning design and layout, coordinating colors and textures, occasionally doing more of the detail work himself. Regardless of where the future takes Alves Contracting, Stephen will continue to find satisfaction in bringing to life what his clients could only imagine.

14

Conquering the Internet

Christopher D. Young, President and COO
Brandy M. Thomas, Chairman and CEO
Cyveillance
Arlington, Virginia

Founded: 1997
1998 Revenues: $800,000
Number of Employees: 46
Initial Investment: $500,000
Current Net Worth: $20 million

I LOVE THIS BUSINESS. This is what I always wanted to do."
Christopher D. Young is speaking both generally and specifically. He and his partner, Brandy M. Thomas, always knew they
would accomplish great things—the specifics they left to the twin
gods of ingenuity and opportunity. Those particular gods are known
to be fickle but with their help, two years ago, Christopher and
Brandy made the first step toward what could well be technology
business history.

Chris, twenty-seven, and Brandy, thirty-one, are early in their careers,
recent graduates of college and graduate school, respectively. For many
people, especially those in the competitive Washington, D.C., metropoli-
tan area, early-career jobs are usually a mere notch above menial professional, the kind of job one endures for the experience and in spite of the
paycheck. But Chris and Brandy, who are no strangers to breaking the
mold, are already high-level executives. Chris is the president and COO
and Brandy the CEO and chair-
man of a $20 million enterprise,
Cyveillance, perhaps the leading
e-business intelligence company
in the industry.

*Net Sapien, the Cyveil-
lance software, represents
an amazing leap forward
in the information
retrieval business.*

With forty-six full-time employees, Cyveillance has revolu-
tionized the ability of companies
to track and protect copyrighted
material, trademarks, and images
on the Internet, where stealing
information is as easy as picking fruit off a tropical tree. Over the past
two years, the company's technical team has created and refined Net
Sapien, patent-pending software (written by Jason Thomas, twenty-
five, Brandy's brilliant younger brother) that continuously scours the
Internet, downloading and indexing more than one million Web pages
and FTP (file transfer protocol) sites each day and searching nearly
45,000 newsgroups. That is what a standard search engine does, but

with one significant difference: Net Sapien has the capacity to conduct surgically precise searches to pinpoint client-focused information and then analyze and prioritize the data according to the client's needs.

The Uncharted Universe

GIVEN that the Internet is analogous to an uncharted universe (the World Wide Web is currently the fastest-growing communications medium, with an estimated 800 million pages of information), searching for pirated material can be like sifting through sand one grain at a time. In that regard, the Cyveillance innovation represents an amazing leap forward in the information retrieval business.

By comparison, competitors operate more like standard news-clipping or monitoring services. They may conduct searches by trademark keyword, for example, "Coca-Cola," but then must sift through every bit of material in which Coca-Cola is mentioned to determine whether a copyright or trademark violation has occurred, an enormously time-consuming approach. Chris draws the comparison this way: "The other guys are strip-mining for information. We are like drillers, going straight for the source."

Business-to-business e-commerce is estimated to reach $300 billion by 2002, a figure that lends weight to Cyveillance's claim that it can prevent billions of dollars in liability and lost sales through its service. The company's own history also supports this claim. Since its inception, Cyveillance has tracked down thousands of cases of unauthorized use of copyrighted material. For example, for a pharmaceutical client, Cyveillance discovered Web sites selling drugs without prescriptions. They routinely find companies falsely claiming to have partnerships with large corporations, and still others using copyrighted names or keywords to divert Internet traffic away from established companies to their less-ethical rivals. Through in-house studies, Cyveillance discovered that at least five hundred different feature films have been illegally offered for sale online, and nearly every cartoon character and feature film star is mentioned or displayed on at least one pornographic site on the World Wide Web.

After some initial growing pains, Cyveillance pulled in $800,000 in its second year of business. On the strength of its exponential growth, Brandy, who concentrates on financing, has had little trouble attracting investors. He has led the Cyveillance team to win the respect and backing of some of the most renowned names in the information technology business. In early 1998, the company attracted an infusion of $3.1 million in venture capital from some heavy hitters in the industry including Lazard Technology Partners of New York and an investor group that includes Virginia-based technology guru Mark Warner and America Online CEO Steve Case. In 1999, the company raised an additional $6.2 million in venture funding from New Enterprise Associates of Menlo Park, California.

> "*The other guys are strip-mining for information. We are like drillers, going straight for the source.*"

Chris, who heads company sales efforts, is equally talented. Under his leadership, Cyveillance achieved a one-thousand percent growth in sales in the first year and a half in business.

The success of Cyveillance is impressive by any measure, but perhaps it is more so because the venture was conceived and is headed by two very young, very self-assured African American men.

Brandy and Chris are walking contradictions, if one believes the stereotypes that—courtesy of the entertainment media, the evening news, and our own misconceptions—define young black men at the end of the twentieth century. They are neither ex-offenders nor drug dealers, rappers nor ball players. Chris, a graduate of Princeton University, where he double-majored in public policy and economics, turned down acceptance at both the Harvard and Stanford business schools to start Cyveillance. And the maniacally self-driven Brandy holds four undergraduate degrees from Duke University, in math, electrical engineering, biomedical engineering, and computer science, as well as an MBA from Stanford.

Chris and Brandy, by example, belie the expectations of a world in which black men can be physical, entertaining, or criminal, but are rarely regarded as thinking beings. Chris and Brandy are not only thinkers, but brilliantly original ones. Together, they challenge and push each other and, in the course of exchanging ideas, push further, past standard boundaries to a whole new set of possibilities.

From Conception to Realization

BRANDY Thomas and Chris Young met at Mercer Management Consulting in Washington, D.C. Mercer was Chris's first job out of college, while Brandy, who is also a savvy computer scientist and systems engineer, had previously worked at Apple Computer, CSE Index, and Mobil Oil and as an independent MIS (management information systems) consultant. At Mercer, the two worked with clients to formulate strategic vision, map out distribution and marketing strategies, run profitability projections, and analyze new growth businesses. Each was making a six-figure salary and doing a fair amount of high-tech management consulting. Both were promoted during their tenure at Mercer. Both wanted to own their own business.

As interest in the Internet caught fire, their Mercer clients started to discuss how the new technology fit into their business strategies, conversations that led Brandy and Chris—already exploring in late-night talks ideas about branching out on their own—to consider a variety of ideas for Internet-based companies. They settled at one point on an Internet-licensing venture. Then it occurred to them to take a step back and consider the real needs of companies beginning to conduct business over the unregulated, vast, and wide-open Internet.

"The idea came that you have to protect before you can license," said Brandy, especially since much of the intellectual property on the Internet is proprietary and vulnerable. It so happened that his MIT-educated brother, Jason, was already designing new search-and-target software, which solidified the nature and direction of the new business.

Upon finding that gap between unmet need and demand, Chris and Brandy began the search for money. One guardian angel appeared in the guise of Dennis Brownlee. Brownlee, himself a successful entrepreneur who sat on Princeton's Board of Trustees with alumnus Chris, believed enough in the two men, their idea, and their ability to see it through to give them office space, computers, and a little bit of money. They borrowed some more from Brandy's in-laws, Milton and Nancy Livingston (also successful entrepreneurs), and supplied the rest from their own savings. With Jason Thomas signed on as vice president of technology and Mark Bildner as vice president of operations, Cyveillance (then Online Monitoring Services) was born in the winter of 1997.

Chris turned down acceptance at both the Harvard and Stanford business schools to start Cyveillance. Brandy holds four undergraduate degrees and an MBA.

They lost money in the first nine months, about $500,000 among the four founders. Client negotiations seemed to drag on endlessly, meaning that money was delayed coming in. Things were uncertain, and the Cyveillance team questioned their commitment to a business they were basically making up as they went along. They all considered quitting. What stopped them was that they never all considered quitting at the same time. When one would say, "I'm not sure we can do this," someone else would say, "Sure we can." The fact that they had each other to lean on kept the momentum going through times when they could barely determine the next step.

Still, Brandy remembers thinking in the beginning, "This is not what I want to be doing"—a reflection less on his faith in the business than on the prudence of having left a well-paying job and security for a venture that was largely unpredictable, with obstacles that were hard to anticipate. Entrepreneurship is always a risk, but what they were doing was tantamount to stepping out on a high wire without spotters or a safety net. Unlike with a car dealership, a hair salon, or a real estate company, there was absolutely no paradigm for Cyveillance to follow.

"There were no minority set-asides [government subsidies], no role models for a business like this," says Brandy. "We're defining it as we go along. We've adapted rapidly and we're good at knowing what we don't know and then finding how to fill the knowledge gap quickly." Adds Chris: "We demand high-quality work from everyone. And we're hard on people because we're hard on ourselves."

In the end, the two decided to move forward instead of standing still to dwell on whether or not they had made the right decision in forming the company. "You have to set objectives and take a risk," explains Brandy. "And you have to accept failure. If you're not failing, you're not pushing." The trick, he adds as an afterthought, is not to fail in the same way twice. What made the critical difference at this turning point was the realization that they had created a product with tremendous value and sky's-the-limit potential.

Chris gave up his apartment and moved in with roommates, and Brandy cut back his lifestyle significantly. What was once taken for granted—that they could buy virtually whatever they wanted—was no longer an option. They put all of their money, time, and thought into the business. Chris focused on clients, and Brandy concentrated on capital.

> *Entrepreneurship is always a risk, but what they were doing was tantamount to stepping out on a high wire without spotters or a safety net.*

Working connections they've made over a few short years, Chris has managed to build an impressive client list that includes the Motion Picture Association of America, Ford Motor Company, Time-Inc.-New Media, the National Basketball Association, and the Software Publishers Association. They reportedly have met with nearly every Hollywood studio, including potential client Dreamworks SKG, the Spielberg-Katzenberg-Geffen powerhouse that is the genius behind blockbuster films such as *Saving Private Ryan.*

No company today can know exactly how its brand, products, images, or information is being used in cyberspace but, according to Cyveillance, nearly eighty percent of Fortune 1000 companies are victims of copyright and trademark misuse on the Internet. Not everybody is happy with the news that their property is frighteningly insecure.

Chris reportedly shocked director Steven Spielberg with a demonstration of how easy it is to download *Saving Private Ryan*—for free. Chris showed him how, with a few clicks of a mouse, Dreamworks SKG stands to lose millions in unrealized profits. "This is the kind of thing that keeps people like Steven Spielberg up at night," Chris commented after the meeting. "I think [he's] a little upset with me right now," adds Chris, speculating that Spielberg is less than happy to have seen just how vulnerable their products are to theft.

Unfortunately, the numbers speak for themselves. Cyveillance has identified sites containing more than 800,000 illegal music files, 600,000 sites with pirated software, and more than 500,000 sites containing pirated videos. Some potential clients find that reality overwhelming.

"Companies can no longer hide their heads in the sand and ignore the mounting issues presented by the Internet," says Brandy. "While the opportunities are great, the risks are even greater." Cyveillance offers a service that likely will become standard operating procedure for businesses whose bottom line is tied inextricably to intellectual property distributed through unregulated media. One way to look at it, offers Brandy, is that if Spielberg hires Cyveillance, he'll be able to get some sleep.

Failure Is Not an Option

ONE trait Brandy and Chris share is that their expectations of themselves have always been as high as, if not higher than, those of the people around them. Both top-level students who excelled in school, they had supportive families and friends who were certain they would achieve wonderful things. While such achievement was important to both of them, the primary goal of each was never to perform below their personal standards.

Chris grew up in Cleveland Heights, Ohio, a working- to middle-class suburb of Cleveland. His father worked at Chrysler and his mother worked at Children's Hospital, sold real estate, and babysat to help support the family. Chris describes his mother as the rock, the arbiter of morals and values in the fam-

> *"You have to set objectives and take a risk. And you have to accept failure. If you're not failing, you're not pushing."*

ily. It is from her, he reports, that he learned the work ethic that keeps him in the office ten, twelve, fifteen hours a day, seven days a week.

While his mother may have lit the flame, Chris cultivated the fire to succeed. Although he was subject to the same pitfalls that threaten all young black men in urban America, he felt from an early age that it was important to follow his internal barometer. He never feared being labeled a nerd or a smart kid who "acted white." Instead, he was proud of the accomplishments that led to him graduating from high school second in his class and won him entrance with a substantial financial aid package to Princeton, his first choice for college.

Brandy was born in Scotch Plains, New Jersey, and attended a preparatory school there until his parents moved the family to Fairfax, Virginia, expressly to allow their sons to take advantage of Fairfax's excellent education system, one of the best in the country. Like Chris, Brandy describes his background as working to middle class. His father was employed at Mobil Oil and his mother worked in real estate.

The move to Virginia was a positive one for Brandy, who attended W. T. Woodson High School, renowned for its science, math, and Latin programs. He took college-level math classes in his junior and senior years and developed an interest in computer programming early on, as did his brother Jason. In the academically competitive atmosphere of Woodson, where he "was a geek who didn't know [he] was a geek," Brandy was impelled to excel. "I have high expectations, but across the board I've intentionally been around people who are better than me because I wanted people to push me."

Chris received an equal amount of support from his high school friends at largely black Cleveland Heights High School. "It was definitely uncool to be smart, but for some reason my friends thought it was cool I was smart. They actually shielded me from trouble in high school because they thought I was risking my future," muses Chris. "My friends respected me for being motivated. But these are guys who had kids right out of high school."

Education experts claim that the absence of peer pressure to do well in school may be responsible for the achievement gap between African American and white students.

Some friends, young African American men as smart as he, sat beside him in elementary school and advanced junior high school classes. As the years went by, however, when Chris looked to either side, he saw fewer and fewer of his friends, until finally they were gone. "By high school, they were barely making it through," Chris says with sadness.

Education experts claim that the absence of peer pressure to do well in school may be responsible for the achievement gap between African American and white students. Certainly, having supportive friends helped both Chris and Brandy close that gap. By the time Brandy graduated from Woodson, he had been president of the high school National Honor Society and was in the top twenty percent of his class with a 3.8 grade point average.

In college, positive peer pressure again made both men strive harder and reach higher. "Among my peers in college, failure was not an option," notes Chris, adding that his classmates at Princeton be-came his role models. The same was true for Brandy at Duke and again in graduate school at Stanford. Their fellow students helped them to keep their eyes on the prize. They were African Americans who displayed not only a fierce desire to achieve but an ease at fitting in at upper-echelon, majority-white schools that had not traditionally been completely open or welcoming to black students and where many African American students had felt uncomfortable in the past.

Chris saw Princeton as an opportunity to open as many doors as possible, to experience life among people of different ethnic back-grounds, different economic circumstances, different philosophies and beliefs. He also saw quite a few African American education casu-alties at Princeton, but they differed from those he had witnessed in high school. The experience was a cautionary one. "As a black stu-dent, you experience all the problems other freshmen face, but it's compounded. You feel like you only have a certain number of people among whom you can feel comfortable, culturally and socially. But I refused to let alienation be a problem," says Chris.

For Chris, the assertive desire to take a place at the table became a largely unconscious mandate to seek out those places where blacks were not traditionally welcome. He lived with white roommates at Princeton and, perhaps most notably, joined the Cap & Gown Eating Club. Eating clubs were once the college equivalent of race-exclusive country clubs and have only in the past decade-and-a-half largely opened membership to women, people of color, and Jews.

For Chris, Cap & Gown did not represent the equivalent of storming the Bastille and was instead simply part of his desire to widen his circle of friends, to broaden his horizons. "I can't live my life in one world," comments Chris, as casually as he lets it be known that his mother is white and his father is black.

"White people were not just characters on television; they weren't a science experiment for me," said Chris, although his openness does not blind him to the reality of racism. While he has rarely been the direct target of racism, he has overheard racist comments that make him cringe and seen the crippling impact of racism on others, and he is hyperaware of its ability to strike forcibly without warning.

For Brandy, fitting in yielded a separate set of issues. He had no trouble feeling comfortable with white folks, having grown up in a mostly white community in Fairfax. The first time he had the opportunity to hang out with a group of blacks for an extended period was at Duke. In addition to learning how to be part of this group, he also needed to learn that there was more to life than studying. At Duke he pledged Omega Psi Phi fraternity, which opened up his social life, a trend he continued at Stanford by going to parties and basically learning how to balance with down time his tendency to be in perpetual forward motion.

> *Adaptability and flexibility are especially important traits for a venture that constantly requires Chris and Brandy to think on their feet.*

Their experiences, both educational and social, helped broaden and prepare Brandy and Chris for any business challenges they might meet. Internally driven, rather self-contained men, they have learned adaptability. This trait, along with its close relative flexibility, the capacity to go with the flow, is especially important for a venture that constantly requires them to think on their feet.

Race, Business, and Opportunity

ALTHOUGH they view it from different vantage points, race has not been something that either Chris or Brandy thought would prevent them from doing whatever they wanted, when they were growing up or now.

"I don't feel like people don't want to deal with me or are uncomfortable with me. I've never gotten a reaction to being black in this business," says Chris. "But it happens to my friends all the time," he adds.

Brandy has a slightly different take on it. "When we walk into the room, there are definitely shocked faces," he says. But he believes the concept and what Cyveillance has to offer overcome any concerns raised by race. "When I walk out of the room, my hope is that it is a small factor, that they say, 'they know what they're talking about,' and that they hire us because we have the solution to the problem."

Brandy and Chris regard themselves as beneficiaries of sacrifices made by their parents, who represent a generation dedicated to opening doors for their children. The two men take the responsibility born of that dedication seriously, not just in terms of their own performance but also in their philosophy about business, the black community, and the idea of giving something back. Both are hopeful that their generation is moving away from the habit of seeing race first and drawing assumptions about character or capability based on color.

They are supporters of anything that helps young African Americans succeed. In their view, this includes affirmative action, self-initiative (the proverbial pulling oneself up by the bootstraps), and their own personal efforts in this area. They see all three as equally important.

"We [African Americans] often lack not only motivation, but a commitment to our community and each other," says Chris, adding that it is a tough issue because black job candidates in the technology field are often scarce. Brandy and Chris believe that qualified black candidates are out there or waiting to be made. Potential is key, and they are willing to act as mentors, both directly and by example, in the same way that their peers in school spurred them to greater achievements.

> "*Today* we are starting to see African Americans excel in corporate America. It's an incredible time because there are so many shifting business paradigms."

"This is the first time that we are really starting to see African Americans excel in corporate America," says Brandy. "We want [Cyveillance] to be big, but we also want to provide an opportunity for the next generation. Now is an incredible time because there are so many shifting business paradigms."

What's Ahead

THE quest for personal wealth is not what drives the founders of Cyveillance. "We're not here to make a million dollars; we could have done that in corporate America," says Brandy, although wealth is a happy by-product of their efforts. "We're here to blow the doors off." Chris elaborates: "We want to have one of the most successful Internet businesses in the world, bigger than Yahoo," he says, citing one of the largest and most profitable Internet portals in the business.

It seems they will have their way. With Net Sapien, Cyveillance will revolutionize the ability of businesses to protect previously vulnerable proprietary information and products, which means that they will help e-businesses survive and profit, a monumental contribution to commerce in the next millennium.

A long-term vision is important to both men, as is the desire to build something bigger than each of them individually, to leave a permanent legacy. Since they've created a unique software, able to do something no other software can, they could indeed become a recognized power in the information industry, one of the biggest Internet businesses in the world, and guarantee themselves a place in history as 'Net pioneers.

Neither can predict what the future holds beyond Cyveillance, although Chris has an interest in electoral politics and Brandy thinks he might like one day to be the CEO of a large corporation. For now, they are focused on the brick-by-brick construction of Cyveillance, expanding the business and staking a bigger claim on the Internet frontier.

Mojo Highway Is a Rough Road to Success

Lee M. Chapman III, Chairman and CEO

Curtis J. Lewis II, President and COO

Mojo Highway Brewing Company, LLC

New York City/Washington, D.C.

Founded: 1998

1998 Revenues: $800,000

Number of Employees: 3

Initial Investment: $40,000

Current Net Worth: $3 million

MOJO HIGHWAY GOLDEN ALE is tagged as "the perfect detour." The slogan is intended to evoke the image of the upscale beer drinker who has been searching for a fresh taste in a stale and stagnant beer market. But the billing is also an apt metaphor for the company's struggle to get off the ground.

Founders of the first African American–owned brewing company in the nation, aspiring tycoons Lee M. Chapman III, twenty-eight, and Curtis J. Lewis II, twenty-nine, began Mojo Highway Brewing Company as a graduate school project after Lee returned from holiday in England in 1994 with the idea of starting his own microbrewery. Somewhere between the research phase and the finished 300-page business plan, setting up a viable brewing company became an obsession. Why?

"Because we said we were going to do it," answers Curtis.

It took five painful and uncertain years to make Mojo Highway a thriving business. Unanticipated obstacles along the way threatened to derail the project, but Lee and Curtis persevered with a focus bordering on the pathological.

The Mojo Highway story is a lesson in intestinal fortitude, or what *Black Enterprise* publisher Earl Graves calls the "junkyard dog mentality" that all black entrepreneurs need in order to succeed. Like pit bulls, Lee (chairman and CEO), Curtis (president and COO), and their vice president of corporate affairs, Celeste Beatty, latched on to the notion of Mojo Highway and refused to be shaken loose. Now the brewing company has offices in New York City and Washington, D.C. Mojo Highway Golden Ale, its super-premium signature brew, is available in fifty high-end bars and restaurants in the D.C./Baltimore area (its test market). The owners are preparing to launch the beer in the New York market, with the rest of the East Coast to follow.

It Seemed Like a Good Idea at the Time

IN the summer of 1994, Lee, an investment banker (he inherited the profession from his father and still does it full-time four days a week), took a much-needed vacation in England. He had little desire to see Buckingham Palace, the London Bridge, or Westminster Abbey. All he wanted to do was visit Burton-Upon-Trent, in the Midlands two and a half hours north of London, home to the Bass Brewery and Lee's then-favorite ale.

Upon arriving at the brewery, Lee discovered it was closed for tours. He patiently explained that he had flown all the way from New York for the specific purpose of touring the plant and simply could not leave without having that dream fulfilled. The result was a private tour, conducted by none other than the vice president of marketing. On his way back to Victoria Station, staring out the train window at the bucolic countryside and crying because he was unhappy in his career, Lee made a decision. He would start his own brewery.

Curtis and Lee had what Black Enterprise *publisher Earl Graves calls the "junkyard dog mentality" that all black entrepreneurs need in order to succeed.*

"I have a passion for beer," he thought at the time. "I want to do this. I *can* do this!" Back in the United States, he immediately called long-time friend Curtis Lewis, who was in graduate school at American University in Washington, D.C. They had both been finance majors at historically black Morehouse College in Atlanta, Georgia, where they had formed a lifelong bond in a particularly brutal finance course. This, said Lee, would be the perfect venture for them. Curtis, another beer aficionado and ever the trend watcher, had noticed that there was a growing diversification of available beer on the market, an indication that the old-line standards such as Budweiser, Coors, and Miller might be losing their lock on the beer market.

Microbreweries (small-scale breweries as compared to the big three: Anheuser-Busch, Miller, and Coors) and specialty microbrews or craft beers (pilsners, ales, and lagers, as well as the more gourmet beers with offbeat twists, such as raspberry ale and mocha porter) were popping up all over. Microbrews made in smaller batches with higher-quality ingredients, tend to be more complex, and usually involve a more time-consuming process than mass-produced beer. American-made microbrews are often on a par with imports. Microbreweries produce fewer than 15,000 barrels a year, and their products are therefore more select and more expensive. Large breweries, on the other hand, are in the business of producing as much beer for as many people as possible (Anheuser-Busch produced 93 million barrels in 1993). The mega-brewers may use cheaper ingredients such as corn or rice instead of barley malt and may scrimp on hops to save money. The end product, according to beer aficionados, is a drink that appeals to the masses but cannot compare with many microbrews and imports.

With microbreweries on the rise, perhaps the time was right to introduce something fresh and new. Intrigued with Lee's idea, Curtis suggested that, since he was in his last year of graduate school, they research their microbrewery venture as an independent study project. They could perform due diligence for the brewery business and Curtis could get school credit for it. While researching and writing the business plan, doing the industry and market analysis, and figuring out operations, long-term

The Mojo team took a shot at what they thought was surefire success. There was only one problem. No one would give them any money.

development, and the specifics of the pro forma financials, they began to believe that this idea had real promise as a viable business.

Their intention was to create a super-premium (higher-quality, higher-priced) beer and market it directly to the hottest and most influential demographic segment of the beer-buying public—the up-scale urban consumer. Lee and Curtis would launch the product in Atlanta, which held appeal for several reasons, one being that the

1996 Olympics would soon be coming to town. "The microbrewery revolution had taken hold in every part of the country with the exception of the Southeast," says Lee. "Atlanta, capital of the 'New South' and a hotbed of new business creation, was prime territory, particularly for a business and product which would be inclusive of an affluent African American market."

It didn't hurt that they already knew their way around the city from their undergraduate days at Morehouse. Armed with brains, initiative, and an ambitious business plan, Curtis and Lee settled on the name Mojo Highway (from a song by jazz fusionist Mark Johnson) and took a shot at what they thought was surefire success.

Roadblock

THERE was only one problem. No one would give them any money. Part of the reason, Lee and Curtis speculate, is that changing circumstances—changes in the market, in beer-drinking trends, and in their own requirements and financial projections—made the business too much of a moving target. Elaborating on the reluctance of financiers, the earnest and contemplative Curtis adds, "We also were too young and too inexperienced." What they lacked in experience, they made up for in chutzpah. It was a quality they would need a lot of in the years ahead.

The partners had envisioned obtaining the rights to a unique-tasting gourmet beer recipe and building a facility, financed by investors, from the ground up. They would make their first product and then expand the line to include more exotic brews. The market, they believed, was there. But while the market was ready, they weren't. "This is when I knew we were in trouble," recalls Lee. "We lost our first-to-market advantage in Atlanta. The opportunity was passing us by, and fast. We were small, with no capital, and every regional specialty brewer, from the likes of the Boston Brewing Company to Redhook, was going public. What's more, AB, Miller, and Coors were introducing their own pseudo craft beers."

From their standpoint, that resulted in two problems. First, they had to drop from the business plan the part about introducing several spin-offs of the original beer, which meant yet another revision. Second, each revision also entailed a recalculation of the financial needs and expectations. Curtis and Lee learned in due course that marketing a craft beer with eight variations, or "line extensions"—such as pilsner, stout, and lager, each a different type of beer—would be logistically impossible. There would be no physical room on store shelves for eight different kinds of Mojo Highway beer. Sellers wouldn't carry them. Lee postulated that it was far easier to build a brand in consumers' minds and gain shelf presence, or recognition, by offering one type of Mojo.

> *What they lacked in experience, they made up for in chutzpah. It was a quality they would need a lot of in the years ahead.*

The dream of an Atlanta launch in time to take advantage of all those thirsty Olympic ticket holders passed them by. Lee and Curtis, who claim to love doing spreadsheets and business plans for fun, would have plenty of opportunity for that brand of enjoyment over the next few years because the research and development phase was only beginning.

Plan Versus Reality

CURTIS and Lee readily admit that they knew nothing about operating a beer company. Their learning curve would span four years. They traveled and drank beer, drank beer and talked to brewers, drank beer and researched the manufacturing process, drank beer and refined the concept, revised the business plan, and tried in vain to find venture capital for the business that had not quite gelled yet, even on paper.

They became obsessed with learning everything they could about beer and how to sell it. Lee says he was particularly possessed. He watched television, read mainstream magazines, and listened to the radio to study and analyze the beer competition's marketing strategies and promotions. He read every trade magazine and online database he could find. He studied and memorized selling and consumption trend data, which he still does today.

During this process, they were not only looking for ways to finance the construction of a brewery; they were looking for product. Beer recipes are licensed in much the same way other intellectual properties are, so they were searching for a flavor they would love enough to buy the rights to it, a beer with a distinctive taste. They figured that if they tasted enough beer, they would stumble upon some obscure beer, waiting, like undiscovered talent, to be made famous.

In 1996, two significant events took place. Lee and Curtis met Celeste Beatty, who became an investor and is currently vice president of corporate affairs, and they found the unique taste they were looking for when they crossed paths with Bill Newman, formerly of Newman Brewing Company in Albany, New York. Having grown tired of the business, Newman had contracted it out, but he retained the rights to his recipe for a smooth amber lager. Curtis and Lee liked it immensely. They negotiated a deal and Mojo Highway bought the rights under the condition that they would alter the recipe from a lager (light, crisp flavor) to an ale (heavier and darker).

Mojo Highway was still a long way from a shelf-ready product, however. Shortly after finding the beer of their dreams, Lee had a meeting with the director of marketing at Seagram Company, which served as the unwitting catalyst for further reconstruction of the Mojo plan. While the director was impressed with the breadth and depth of Lee's knowledge as well as his confidence, he turned down the request for capital because the company was too small.

"I walked out of the meeting with Seagram's with even a stronger will," says Lee. "I had just had a twenty-plus-year veteran of the beverage industry tell me I was awesome. I was literally fifty feet from Sea-gram's when it hit me. Put Mojo in a green bottle, differentiate it from craft beer, and essentially create a new beer category. Mojo would have the feel and complexity of a craft/specialty beer, the look and price of an import beer, and the youthfulness and personality of a domestic specialty beer, effectively filling the void between craft/spe-cialty and import beer brands."

In the beer business, the difference between the green and brown bottle is like the difference between a Giorgio Armani original and a dollar-store suit. While the green bottle says "import," the brown bot-tle is associated with domestic beer and, horror of horrors, malt liquor, the kind of beer more likely to be drunk out of a brown paper bag on the street than from a frosted mug at the corner bistro. Mojo Highway, the brewers wanted everyone to understand, is most em-phatically not malt liquor—not Colt 45, not Olde English, not Red Bull. Hence, the packaging becomes key. The decision to put Mojo in a green bottle may seem an obvious one, but in the U.S. beer industry the brown bottle is standard for all beers, while imports come in the green bottle. Curtis and Lee were breaking with tradition.

> *In the beer business, the difference between the green and brown bottle is like the difference between a Giorgio Armani origi-nal and a dollar-store suit.*

What Lee actually did was shift the branding (making the brand name recognizable) and other marketing strategies of Mojo away from ingredient-based hyperbole that craft beers use ("made from Rocky Mountain spring water") to a selling concept known as "aspirational" marketing ("drink this and everyone will know you have good taste and can afford the expense"). The import-style green bottle is a visual cue that the product is more refined, that it speaks the language of the upscale "urban" buyer. "Urban" in this usage does not refer exclusively to blacks and Latinos (as the word used to imply), but to a class of image-conscious, well-heeled, educated professionals as likely to be white as black and suburban as urban. Think the cast of *Living Single, Love Jones,* or *Ally McBeal.* Upwardly mobile Generation X and GeneratioNext consumers who shop at Barney's, drive a BMW, dine at expensive restaurants. They are sophisticated buyers who can afford to pay for status with a capital S. They are, as Curtis described them to a Washington weekly, "VPs by day, hip-hop, extreme sports junkies by night."

According to Lee, the new marketing and branding strategy—the combination of the green bottle and "aspirational" marketing—was the epiphany that took Mojo Highway to another conceptual level, placing it in direct competition with the fastest-growing segment of the beer industry: the imports. The bottle would transform the beer to high-end status, to Cinderella at the ball as opposed to the dirty-faced dreamer by the fire.

"I Like It, But . . ."

MEANWHILE, the intrepid Celeste Beatty, scion of a well-connected family in North Carolina, had been refining the art of cold-calling potential investors and convincing them to meet with the Mojo Highway principals. In the search for money, she contacted an exhaustive list of private investors, venture capitalists, and admitted long-shots, including Bill Cosby and Will Smith.

Curtis and Lee had traveled from Seattle to Atlanta visiting breweries, seeking wisdom and advice and to see how others were achieving what they hoped to do. Four years into their venture, the two had talked to 200 to 250 potential investors and every affluent person they could find, including friends, family, and every black venture capital firm or individual. Banks were out of the question because they had nothing to collateralize.

Every contact had a reason to turn them down. Some said they were too young and didn't know enough about the brewery business. Lee takes great exception to that conclusion. "Every beer or beverage executive that we talked to, especially the ones I saw, were truly impressed with my knowledge," he says. "Moreover, we planned to sell Mojo to a demographic that we represent. Who better to sell beer to this group than us?"

Financiers were unconvinced. Some advised them to bring on an older and white partner experienced in the industry to inspire investor confidence. (They wouldn't.) They heard again and again from potential money people that a brewery "just doesn't fit my [investment] profile" and that it was "too risky" or, interestingly, that the amount they asked for was not enough. They came to expect the "no." "If you don't have money or anything to leverage, you make your first deal off investments from family and friends," comments Curtis.

It was frustrating and painful for the partners to hear "no" from African American business owners and investors. They approached everybody from the Rainbow Coalition/PUSH, founded by Jesse Jackson, to rap mogul Sean "Puff Daddy" Combs and Robert Johnson, CEO of Black Entertainment Television. "A lot of [black] people we approached were used to putting their money into the tried and true," says Curtis. "A barber shop, a deli. There are not a lot of blacks in manufacturing. We have car dealerships, franchises, we sell haircare products."

While they didn't get money, they got a lot of advice from successful black entrepreneurs. Many were cautiously optimistic, many suggested they give up on the brewery idea and try something else. A few beverage company executives tried to hire Lee, and one potential investor told Curtis he "couldn't make money selling beer and should join him and do government contracting." Curtis was not tempted. "I have no passion for that," he told the man.

The New Power Generation

PASSION is something the duo is unwilling to sacrifice. They are definitely part of what's being popularly termed "the new power generation," young blacks who never knew the kind of restrictions and limitations their parents faced. Unfettered by the encompassing overt racism of the past, they are used to going where they want, doing what they want, and having their expectations met.

"We're not held down by that traditional thinking," explains Curtis, adding that, while they found it disappointing, they understood the reluctance of traditional investors to support a venture like Mojo Highway. "If you come from three generations of businessmen who make concrete blocks, you're not supposed to sell books over the Internet."

Lee, less diplomatic, attributes the African American business community's lack of investor interest to myopia. "They can't think outside the box," he says. "African Americans habitually wait until an idea or concept is championed by someone else, usually a white someone else, before we endeavor. We are too damn risk averse."

> *Curtis and Lee are part of "the new power generation," young blacks who never knew the kind of restrictions and limitations their parents faced.*

Perhaps this new generation of black entrepreneurs is at a crossroads in some respects. They grew up witnessing the entrepreneurial spirit at work. Lee's father was the first African American managing director at Equitable Life Assurance Society and went on to found Chapman and Associates, an investment concern. Curtis's father, an attorney and owner of Curtis Lewis and Associates law firm, previously ran a jewelry-making business and made and sold leather bags (his hobby). Their sons' generation wants to take entrepreneurship to the next level, but, as they and other young black entrepreneurs maintain, black investor confidence has not kept pace with change.

That may be more a function of caution toward new economic developments in society in general than a characteristic specific to African Americans. In matters of money, finance, and the economy, conservatism is often the norm. Maybe black investors tend to be more conservative, or maybe Lee and Curtis were just the wrong people with the wrong qualifications knocking on the wrong doors.

Whatever the reason for their failure to find money, the delay gave them time to refine their venture and its final product: the first domestically brewed, super-premium ale sold in an import-style green bottle.

Mojo Takes Off

THE significance of the green bottle cannot be overstated. It was what eventually put Mojo over the top. At the end of five years, in 1998, Curtis and Lee had met with nearly everybody they could remotely think of as a possible source of financing. As they followed up on some contacts for the umpteenth time, they got to talking with Steve Nordall of the Frederick Brewing Company, a NASDAQ-listed venture in Frederick, Maryland, and the first brewery they had toured.

Frederick Brewing is one of the largest breweries in the mid-Atlantic region and Nordall, vice president of operations, had been a source of inspiration and information throughout the long and painful effort to bring Mojo Highway to fruition. In June of 1998, Frederick, which went public in 1995, was doing well and had just acquired two more brewing companies. Curtis and Lee thought, "What the hell?" The word "no" has a way of opening the mind to new possibilities and different ways of doing things. So they asked if Frederick might be interested in contract brewing Mojo Highway, meaning they would contract Frederick to brew Mojo Highway at its facility. In this way, Curtis and Lee would save the expense and effort of building a brewery and running its operation.

To their delight, Nordall and Marjorie McGuinness, president of Frederick Brewing Company, were intrigued at the idea of making a new beer and pitching it to a whole new segment of the market, especially as the Mojo partners thought they could easily sell 10,000 barrels of ale annually. To put that in context, for a small company to sell 2,000 to 3,000 barrels a year is considered a successful year.

Curtis and Lee based their number on the fact that they would be selling to a demographic that had been overlooked and undervalued by beer sellers in the past. And they were launching the product in the Washington, D.C., area, home to a large affluent African American population completely willing to spend more than $5 for a bottle of beer.

After various revisions to the business plan, Frederick Brewing contracted to brew Mojo Highway for a twenty-five percent share of the company and an initial investment from Lee, Curtis, and Celeste of $40,000 (significantly less than the $800,000 they had sought to build a brewery from the ground up). As part of the deal, Mojo Highway would be distributed through Kronheim Distributors.

In August of 1998, Mojo Highway Brewing Company debuted its Golden Ale at the trendy Republic Gardens club on U Street at the epicenter of D.C. urban nightlife. They had sent out three thousand invitations and done a bit of radio promotion, but word of mouth must have been buzzing—the line for the launch party wrapped around the block. They sold 1,600 bottles, an incredible amount for one brand in one night.

Mojo Highway was launched and the Mojo team shifted its attention to promotion and sales. They hand-picked the venues where Golden Ale would be available, focusing on northwest D.C. and Georgetown bars—upper-end D.C., the equivalent of New York's Greenwich Village. Mojo is unavailable in some working-class areas of Washing-

In beer marketing, attitudes about race are so rooted in stereotypes that the campaigns are more likely to alienate than attract the black community.

ton, a purely strategic decision, according to Lee. "We only want to place our brand where it's going to get us the most value for our dollar. At a certain point, it becomes an economic equation," he told Washington's *City Paper.* As off-putting as that may sound, his point is strongly imbedded in the marketing history of beer. Traditionally, beer marketing has been all about image, projecting a certain profile, and appealing to certain qualities in the target market.

The Mojo partners are going for the same urban demographic targeted by Tommy Hilfiger, Donna Karan, and FUBU, a stratum that has only recently gained the attention of demographers and companies and been largely ignored in this context by beer makers. This approach represents a whole new way of looking at beer marketing in an industry in which the attitudes about race and who buys particular brands of beer are so rooted in stereotypes that the campaigns are more likely to alienate than attract certain segments of the black community. For example, malt liquor ads, which suggest that their fortified product enhances sexual prowess, are considered crude by the urban crowd, who are looking for a more refined drink.

Fortified alcohol malt liquors have long been packaged for and pitched heavily to a stratum of the inner-city market. The image is all about power, virility, and strength: picture the snorting, charging bull on the Red Bull label and the bucking bronco of Colt 45 fame. One brand threw away all pretense and just said it explicitly: "Gets your girl in the mood quicker and makes your jimmie thicker." All are designed to suggest that you can be bigger, badder, and better if you drink _____ (fill in the blank).

The Mojo crew is attempting to sell a new product to a new market. The major domestic brewers are intent on keeping their customers and selling them on line extensions as they are introduced. Rarely is there a concerted effort to reach beyond the comfort zone of the mass market, which is less likely to be as selective as import or microbrew drinkers. If "urban" consumers fall into the mass market, fine. But mega-brewers have not really discovered or pursued the "urban" demographic. Mega-brewers only reach the urban market by default, rather than targeting them as a primary consumer. Lee and Curtis are taking advantage of the industry's slowness to reach out specifically to the new urban consumer and are staking a claim before other beer companies get hip to the possibilities.

The Mojo principals, who believe in applying the personal touch to promotion, are likely to show up at a restaurant or bar and talk to patrons, telling them about Mojo Highway firsthand, even going so far as to gently remove a bottle of Heineken from a customer's hand and replace it with one of their own. Celeste is particularly notorious for the "Mojo Highway switch," as it has come to be known.

They set up numerous tastings, frequent the clubs and restaurants where Mojo Highway is sold, and meet with beer sellers and distributors to pitch the product. At B. Smith's, a trendy, upscale African American restaurant in Washington's historic Union Station (where Curtis and Lee encountered author and poet Maya Angelou and sold her on Mojo Highway—she really liked it), they sell three to four cases of Mojo Highway a month. Nowhere near Heineken, but not bad.

Mojo management has learned to listen to and apply the advice of people with experience in the beer-selling business. Apparently it takes some romancing to get distributors and liquor store owners to carry a new, upstart product its owners insist must be placed on the shelf next to Heineken and sold for the same price. Such delusions of grandeur (that green bottle again) do little to endear Mojo Highway to doubting publicans

> *The partners pitch their beer to bar patrons, even sometimes gently removing a bottle of Heineken from a customer's hand and replacing it with Mojo.*

way to doubting publicans and others, but Curtis and Lee keep at it. "We had to make promises that we hoped we could keep," says Lee. "It's a hustle. Show commitment, dedication, and attention to your brand, and the retailer will work for you." When they get past the initial skepticism about who they are ("yes, we really do own the company," although Lee has been known to claim, tongue in cheek, that he drives a beer truck), they have been able to do a pretty persuasive job of selling what's in the bottle—as evidenced by growing sales.

Looking Ahead

THE long upward climb was worth it. The company is expected to gross over $1 million in 1999, with future hopes for the brand to be sold in most major U.S. cities. Curtis recently quit his job as a financial analyst to devote all of his time to Mojo Highway. If the New York launch goes as well as planned, perhaps Lee will leave investment banking behind, too.

Curtis and Lee have no idea what they'll do after they turn Mojo Highway into an even more profitable company. They are, in their heart of hearts, businessmen, which means they love the art of creating a business, making it successful, and then moving on to the next challenge.

For the present, they still work sixteen-hour days and weekends pushing Mojo Highway. "Within three years, Mojo will be a very strong brand to rival Corona, Tecate, and Heineken in select cities on a regional basis," predicts Lee, and Curtis concurs. Given their track record for making what they say come true, it's hard not to believe it'll happen.

16

He's Got the Power

James W. Winters II

CEO

United Energy, Inc.

Portland, Oregon

Founded: 1991

1998 Revenues: $60 million

Number of Employees: 52

Initial Investment: $6,000

Power concedes nothing without a demand.
It never has and never will.

—*Frederick Douglass*

S OME FOLKS THINK you have to have a roaring tiger in your tank to succeed in the energy business. James W. Winters II has made it big with a panther on his chest, a vision in his heart, and a surprisingly soft-spoken, but steely determination to do things his way.

As CEO of United Energy, Inc., a petroleum product (fuel and related products) distribution company, James, thirty-seven, is the most successful black entrepreneur in his home state of Oregon. While working as a temp, he founded the company in his living room in 1991, with a $6,000 loan from friend Gregory Allen. United Energy's first rented office was, literally, a broom closet. Today, with $60 million in annual revenues and a staff of fifty-two in an elegant, professional suite of offices, the company is growing fast. With an eye on the future, James and Gregory (that early loan made him a shareholder in the company) are expanding their base from petroleum product distribution to a network of service stations with mini-marts and fast-food chains.

The eight-year-old company is the seventy-fourth largest minority-owned industrial company in the country and has twice been on *Black Enterprise* magazine's list of one hundred top companies. James was featured in a July 1999 *Black Enterprise* cover story on the "New Power Generation." He's also made the front page of Oregon's second-largest newspaper, *Willamette Week.*

High Expectations

EVEN as a child growing up in the predominantly black northeast section of Portland, James was goal oriented. His younger brother Darrell (one of James's three siblings and now United Energy's operations manager) compares their family to the Huxtables, the fictional family made famous on the *Cosby Show.* "We had two professional parents with real strict rules," Darrell recalls. "We had to bring home good grades, had to clean our rooms daily, we had chores lined up and they had to be done. Education in our family was always a priority, always highly stressed."

"Our parents had high expectations," James agrees. Their father, James, Sr., was a schoolteacher with a master's degree, while their mother, Patricia, was an office manager for an architectural firm. Both are now retired.

Darrell remembers James as a "brilliant" child who challenged his teachers and placed schoolwork before fun. "Of course he'd hang with his friends, but he was focused." In James's view, he was only "a slightly above average student, in the middle of the bell curve. You wouldn't have picked me out of the talent pool. I look at a lot of the white people I went to college with. They had the grades and accolades, but I've passed them like they're standing still. It's because they had the academic skills, but I had the determination."

> *Even as a child growing up in the predominantly black northeast section of Portland, James was goal oriented.*

Even as a child, he wanted to be a businessman wearing nice suits and carrying a briefcase to work in an office. "That's what my dad wanted me to be. I'm named after him and it just kind of rubbed off." But James just assumed he'd work for someone else. This orientation was inspired in part by talks with his paternal grandfather about the hard life of a laborer. "He told me about how he was a laborer at the railroad for thirty-five years, and the only thing that kept him going was so his kids and grandkids could have better opportunities than he did. He moved his family from Mississippi to Arkansas to Nevada, and then to Oregon in search of better opportunities. He just found a way to get it done."

Understanding how hard his grandfather strove to better his family's opportunities drove James, as did seeing how others lived. "Pimps had Cadillacs, dressed up, hung out. I saw some whites with nice cars, living in nicer houses than ours. I wondered how they could live like that and we had to be pimps to live that way. I always felt determined to live that way without being involved in illegal activities." When folks tried to tempt James beyond the law, he followed his parents' example and stayed on the straight and narrow. "Deep down inside, I always felt that I could make it legitimately."

James's only childhood business venture was to start a shoeshine business, which he shut down when his parents disapproved. "When we had folks over, I'd come out and try to shine everybody's shoes," he recalls. "My parents told me to stop. They said, 'You're not going to be a shoeshine boy. We want you to be something better than that.'"

James watched others with less education and experience vaulting over him. The ceilings he bumped up against were not glass, but concrete.

In the pursuit of something better, James brought home good grades, excelled in athletics, and later earned a degree in business at Oregon State University, "completely expecting to work my way up at IBM or some place like that."

Instead, his first job after graduating was as an accountant at a small machine tool manufacturing company outside Portland. His supervisor, a white man, "was the best mentor that I could have had. He educated me about life in the business world." According to James, his supervisor said to him, "You're very, very talented, James. The business world is not ready for you. You're going to go from company to company and you'll only get promoted so far, because whites just aren't ready and there will be too many politics."

"I told him I was willing to work hard and overcome that," James recalls. The man suggested that James think about starting his own business. "It sounded good, but I didn't have a clue about what kind of business to be in, so I just put it in the back of my mind."

He then went to work for a petroleum corporation in California and Texas, analyzing financial data. The mentor's predictions were fulfilled as James moved from company to company, being promoted once or twice and then watching others with less education and experience vaulting over him. The ceilings he bumped up against were not glass, but concrete, says James.

Breaking Through

ONE too many ceilings prompted him to look into starting his own business, although he had no idea what that would be. "I didn't have a clue. I felt like, whatever God intends. I just knew I couldn't work for somebody else. I thought I might buy an existing business, but I didn't know."

A defining moment came when, at age twenty-nine, James was watching the television show *thirtysomething* and a character said, "Whatever you're doing at thirty, you'll be doing the rest of your life." James decided it was time to get moving and started formulating an action plan. "I knew something about the petroleum distribution chain," says James, so he started thinking hard about that. He went into a popular bar and grill, scribbled possible names for the business on cocktail napkins, and asked the waitress to select one. She chose United Energy. The next day, he made sure the name was available and incorporated the company.

It was September 1991. His parents rented him a house to live in, and he worked a temporary job in the tax department of a freight company to survive. He bought a desk, office chair, and filing cabinet for $50 cash at a garage sale, borrowed a fax machine from his sister, and turned his living room into an office. He'd work all day at the freight company, hit the library to scour business publications and journals for potential clients, and then head home to write pitch letters.

A book about the art of selling taught him that if you make ninety-nine phone calls and one of them is a good one, those are pretty good odds. Each rejection puts you that much closer to someone accepting what you're saying. Still, after eight months with no nibbles, "There were times when I put my head on the desk and said, 'This isn't going to work. I'm going to become a schoolteacher or something,'" remembers James. "But I'd go to sleep on it and wake up with even more determination."

Finally, James called the supplier for a chain of gas stations and said, "If I can sell about seventy barrels of these lubricants a year, will you make me a branded distributor?" Sure, the man agreed, but he couldn't give United Energy any credit, so they'd have to prepay everything. "He gave me the prices. I added a markup and submitted it to the customer." James hadn't bothered to start small. The customer was no nickel-and-dime operation, but the Bechtel Corporation, a global engineering-construction organization headquartered in San Francisco. Bechtel was building a natural gas line from Canada to California and needed motor oil for its machinery. "[Bechtel] called me a week later, ready to place the order."

James scribbled possible names for the business on cocktail napkins and asked the waitress to select one. She chose United Energy.

With one day to fill the order, James faced some serious hitches. "I didn't have anything but my phone, my desk, and my fax machine. I didn't have the lube oil or any way to transport it." Gregory Allen made the loan and James made him a shareholder. Then he rented the biggest truck he could find and hired a college kid to ride with him. The cargo weighed so much that the drive took much longer than planned, but James delivered.

For the next eight months, he continued working as a temp while building his client base and renting trucks when the need arose. Then he rented his first downtown office "because the address would make us look like a bigger company." The only space he could afford was a broom closet, for $75 a month. It was so small he could barely turn around and so stuffy he had to keep the window open year-round. Greg, who worked as a transportation engineer for the city of Portland, dropped by after work to see how things were going.

United Energy's big turning point came in 1992, when James got a contract to supply jet fuel to American Airlines. "We had pelted them with so many letters and phone calls, I think they just gave up and said, 'Here, take some business.'" It didn't take long, though, for American's manager of supplier diversity to be impressed by James's potential and vision of where he wanted to take United Energy.

The contract allowed James to scale back his day job, but though United Energy made $400,000 in sales in its second year, he didn't draw a salary until the business was a year and a half old. "I always felt that the company should have money in the bank, no matter what," he explains. The new contract also enabled James to move the business out of the broom closet to better offices down the hall. The reputation he established with American opened doors with other clients, including United, Delta, National Car Rental, and Alamo.

After watching the market for a year, James decided to expand into home heating oil. He got a line of credit and bought a truck, figuring it would take about eighteen months to pay it off. It took eighteen days. He bought another truck and then faced a new challenge. Carrying three thousand pounds of diesel fuel was dangerous. "If you spilled it, you'd probably be out of business, and you might burn to a crisp, too," James says matter-of-factly. It was so hard to keep drivers that James had to get behind the wheel himself. He recruited brother Darrell, a drummer who worked with talents such as SWV, Atlantic Starr, Tag Team, and CeCe Penniston, to drive the truck between music gigs.

After a few very good years distributing home heating oil, James began to lose business slowly but surely as customers converted from oil heat to natural gas. "That's when we turned to what I call the asset realization mode," says James. "You either acquire or become acquired. We spun off that part of the company, sold it, and concentrated on selling fuel to aviation companies." Darrell became United Energy's full-time operations manager.

In 1994, James learned about a minority enterprise program with the U.S. Department of Transportation, which, he says, "didn't give us new clients but gave the customers we had more incentive to buy from us" because using the minority supplier was helping to fulfill the DOT requirements. When these programs, which were administered by the federal government and run through the states, began to be dismantled at the state level, James knew he better not let the success of his business be dependent on them. James says these programs are "a great way to jump-start your business and get your cash flow going, but you certainly can't get a lifetime of business out of them."

A Commitment to the Community

IN 1998, James began steering United Energy into the consumer market with the nearly million-dollar purchase of a Chevron service station and convenience store in northeast Portland—the 'hood. His goal: to clean up what had been a haven for drinking and drug dealing and provide jobs in the community. Rather than applauding his effort, the city of Portland has continued the "chronic nuisance" lawsuit they had filed against the previous owner, a legal move sometimes used to shut down drug houses.

James is angry that the city is holding him responsible for preexisting problems that he is working to solve. On top of that, he says, the folks who run his hometown are dissing him. According to *Willamette Week,* city officials have called James "a liar and a criminal," opposed his beer and wine license, and made him get an FBI fingerprint check. James doesn't know of any other business owners who have had their fingerprints taken, and a rival gas station less than a mile away is allowed to sell beer to its customers. In early 1999, James filed a federal lawsuit, charging that the city violated his civil rights.

Again according to *Willamette Week,* "The City's case against Winters has more to do with historical problems at the Chevron station that it does with him or his partner. . . . Problems at the corner where the station is located can be traced back to the early '90s, when it was a vacant lot attracting prostitution, drunkenness, drug sales, armed robbery, and other criminal activities."

While James calls the legal maneuvers a distraction and an exercise in futility, he has vowed to fight to the finish. "I would much rather be spending my time doing other things, but I have a responsibility to protect my company's assets. They probably thought this is just a little black company and we'll fold up and go away if they press hard

> *James bought a Chevron station/convenience store in the 'hood. His goal: to clean up a drinking and drug dealing haven, and provide jobs in the community.*

enough, but that hasn't happened. We can't back off. We will continue until we feel these issues have been adequately addressed. Then, we are willing to accept whatever the verdict is."

While keeping his large petroleum clients, James is now focusing on retail as "the future of this company." And, battles with the city over the Chevron station aside, he foresees bright horizons and a continued commitment to his community. He moved his offices from downtown to northeast Portland, hoping, as a role model and neighborhood employer, to inspire black youth. "I just feel that, as an African American, I'd like to see brothers and sisters rise up and take back what's rightfully ours."

A former donor to Democratic causes, James now calls himself a "new Republican" who believes black people are better off without government assistance. "I started out as a Democrat, but I saw a huge difference of philosophy. A lot of people, many of them well meaning, don't understand what it's gonna take for us to rise up as a race of people and share in God's glory and resources. It is not going to come from any government program. The government doesn't have to be involved to make us a success." James did, however, support Democratic efforts to save affirmative action programs.

James is a study in contrasts. His conservatively short haircut is set off by a small gold hoop in each ear. His sharply tailored suit, white shirt, and tastefully expressive tie clothe a panther tattoo on his chest, chosen, he says, because it's the fiercest creature in the wild.

> "*To see the enjoyment and pride on my parents' faces when they read about my accomplishments makes it all worthwhile.*"

The suit is a nod to tradition. The panther speaks more to the real James. "I'm not a typical suit-and-tie person," says James, who often wears baggy jeans and hiking boots to work. "I'm a brother; I'm still just a 'hood rat who managed to get through college."

He and Gregory belong to an otherwise all-white country club that has welcomed them with open arms. There, they enjoy golf and the other perks of success. But James's time away from the job is also devoted to community work. He serves as treasurer of his local Urban League, provides financial support to several local youth programs, hosts a huge charity golf tournament for kids, and speaks at an annual Rotary Club retreat for aspiring young urban entrepreneurs.

The man who says that business "is nothing more than a chess game, except the board is a lot longer," confides that he is "very spiritual about my success. I think that letting God, Christ, come into my life and putting all my trust in him has blessed me. I've had access to God's resources." He attends two nondenominational Christian churches: one black, near his offices and boyhood home; and the other white, located closer to his secluded home near the Oregon-Washington border.

A source of great joy, says James, is "that both my parents are still alive to see this. To see the enjoyment and pride on their faces when they read about my accomplishments makes it all worth-while." As for what he hopes to pass on to the next generation, James states, "I want to be the one who inspired groups of young brothers to go out and use their entrepreneurial skills, reclaim our community. I've had the opportunity to talk to lots of kids, some drug dealers, and they're smart business people. They're just selling the wrong thing. It's a shame because, to me, some of them are absolutely brilliant. If they had grown up in an environment where someone said it's possible for them to make it in legitimate business, they might be somewhere now."

CHAPTER

A Kinder, Gentler Way Out of Debt

Alvin Rice
President
D & R Recovery
Silver Spring, Maryland

Founded: 1992
1998 Revenues: $903,000
Number of Employees: 24–31 (seasonal)
Initial Investment: $100
Current Net Worth: $4 million

"MY DOG ATE my bill." While this excuse may win points for entertainment value, it doesn't change the fact that when debt is outstanding, the bill is still due, says Alvin Rice. Lame excuses aside, founder and president of D & R Recovery—the largest black collection agency in Maryland—is often willing to work with the perpetrators of outrageously bogus attempts to dodge debt. Alvin succeeds where others fail because he brings an alternative philosophy and strategy to the collection business: empathy, education, and responsibility.

"We try to help debtors understand credit," says Alvin. "We want to work with them and teach about resolving debt and the importance of becoming creditworthy." An interesting new tack to follow—reform over dunning—but this velvet glove versus sledgehammer approach can improve what is typically a difficult situation all around. And it has won Alvin some fans in the most unlikely places.

"I thought it was almost a pleasant experience," reported an anonymous debtor with a long-unpaid cable television bill. "They educated me about the collection process and the importance of credit . . . and they never received another late bill from me."

An impressive statement from a reformed deadbeat, but it is something Alvin Rice has become accustomed to hearing. Besides, being in over your head is something he understands. In 1992, he was working for another collection agency, Capital Credit Corporation, when it suddenly went out of business. Broke and feeling powerless, with a wife and a new baby, Alvin packed up his van and went on vacation to visit his grandmother in Alabama. He maxed out his credit cards on that trip and didn't have "two nickels to rub together" when he got back. Whether divine inspiration or the gods of great irony inspired his next professional decision, we'll never know. But when his wife, Angelia, asked him what he was going to do, the man with no money and credit-card debt up to his neck, blurted out: "I'm going to start my own collection agency." Later that year, he did.

Out of only four years of experience in the debt collection industry and $100, D & R Recovery was born. With the $100, Alvin
bought a desk, a database, an old phone, and some software. Today,
the company, based in Silver Spring, Maryland (just outside Washington, D.C.), has a net worth of $4 million, with 1999 revenues esti-
mated at $2.5 million. D & R
has grown from Alvin, a friend,
and Angelia to a staff of between twenty-four and thirty-
one employees depending on
the time of year (just after
Christmas is especially hectic).
Alvin's brother Tim is the marketing director for the company.

> *Alvin maxed out his credit cards and didn't have "two nickels to rub together" before starting his own collection agency.*

D & R numbers among its
clients Bell Atlantic, TCI Com-
munications, and Kaiser Permanente. Working with industry giants
means the company collects money from people all over the country.
Lately, Alvin has been scouting around for other collection agencies to
acquire in the South or on the West Cost and is considering diversification into related areas such as handling telephone overflow for utility or phone companies during crises. He also expects to open a
division of the business in Atlanta soon.

Alvin Rice, thirty-nine, is the antithesis of what one expects a
debt collector to be. He is a humble, genuinely decent guy and a devoted family man who has been married to the same woman for
eighteen years and dotes on his two children, Halston, fourteen, and
Myisha, seven. The question must frequently arise in the minds of
those he encounters in his business: "What's a nice guy like you . . ."

Early Interests

WHEN Alvin Rice was young, growing up in Columbus, Ohio, he
had free-floating, rather amorphous dreams of riches, shaped by his

desire of the moment: he would be an architect or a real estate mogul or perhaps owner of a pro sports franchise.

"I wanted to own the Cleveland Browns," he remembers. "And I was an excellent artist as well. I would ride through downtown Columbus, but I would visualize New York and draw copies of a dome stadium or of a high rise and say to myself 'I'm going to own all of this.'"

At fifteen, he became a dishwasher at Lazarus Department Store. When he started school at Ohio State University, where he majored in accounting, he picked up a job at Lazarus again, this time in retail. He told his mother about his career change, but she was unimpressed.

"I said, 'Mom, you know what? I'm working in retail now.' She said, 'Boy, you need to take that shoestring off your neck and get you a real job working at the post office because that's where the money is.' She just wanted to see him make it and not have to struggle," explains Alvin. His mother knew that the department store would only pay him minimum wage, which at the time was $3.25 an hour. "But something deep inside me told me that you have to start somewhere in order to build it up," says Alvin. He believed in the power of motivation and was a young man who took the lessons life and his parents taught about hard work and perseverance seriously. "My family is from the South and they have always been hard workers—I mean, *hard* workers," he says. "My mother and father would work from sunup to sundown and they instilled in us that you have to get out there and work if you want something. They pushed education just as hard, but the foundation was really on the work ethic."

Alvin is the oldest of three brothers in a close-knit family. In search of a better life for themselves and their sons, his parents moved the family from Alabama to Columbus before Alvin was born. His father worked at Westinghouse for years, and as a custodian. His mother worked for AT&T. They both lived the example they wanted their children to follow. Like many black fathers of their generation, Alvin's father would go to work at six in the morning and get home at 11:30 at night. Although he rarely saw his sons during the week, he made up for it on weekends, just by being there, talking, listening. Alvin's mother did the same and kept her own traditions by cooking the huge Sunday dinner after church when everyone gathered for family time.

"There was so much given to us," says Alvin. "I can never remember a time when the lights were off or bill collectors were calling or never having clothes or not having a roof over our heads."

In addition to providing a nurturing family environment and a strong Baptist foundation, the Rices also emphasized the value of education. Alvin was an average student, as were his two younger brothers, and their parents pushed them all to study harder, with the advice that the more they studied, the better off they would be. But from the time he was eleven or twelve, Alvin was really thinking about how to make money, and not just hourly wage work, but investment and return.

> *At eighteen, Alvin bought his first house, for $4,000, and turned around and sold it for $8,000.*

To that end, at eighteen he bought his first house. He went to his mother and told her that he had his eye on a HUD (Housing and Urban Development) home, a victim of foreclosure that was up for auction. He had been looking at HUD homes since he was sixteen and had finally found one in a rundown section of Columbus that was more in need of cosmetic than expensive structural work. He and his mother made a bargain that she would finance the deal if he paid the monthly note and gave her half the proceeds after he rehabilitated and sold the house. They went to the auction and bought the house for $4,000. But when Alvin's father looked at the house, he discovered that the foundation was unstable. A contractor confirmed Mr. Rice's conclusion. "One thing I learned in doing business is to have whatever you're going to do checked out," says Alvin. "Do your due diligence."

Luck was with Alvin, however, and the incident proved fateful. The contractor who looked at the house offered to buy it for $8,000 and Alvin got a taste of what life was like outside the minimum-wage world. "I said, 'Oh, my God! If I could make this working at La-zarus!" he remembers, and from then on his focus shifted and his perspective on money changed. "This is where I want to be. I want to plug into where the money is," he said at the time.

Alvin deferred that dream even as he thought he was chasing it. To keep money coming in, he worked for the city of Columbus as a sanitation worker for nine years, from the time he was eighteen until he moved to Maryland in 1988. He changed course then and found a job as a unit manager at American Creditors Bureau, moved up to senior collector, and then jumped to the Capital Credit Corporation. All the while, he tried a slew of get-rich-quick schemes.

"I've tried Shaklee, PriAmerica . . . you name it, I've tried it," says Alvin, referring to the multilevel marketing schemes that seduce participants with promises of freedom from money worries. "I tried all those things because I wanted to be financially independent." The move to Maryland was his attempt at a geographical cure to jumpstart his life and dreams. The career switch from sanitation work to debt collection was a beginning, but Alvin was seeking more than just a different job. "I came here [to Maryland] and took a whole different approach."

A New Path

NOT long after Alvin got back from his credit-card road trip, he set up an office in the basement washroom of his home and launched D & R Recovery. His wife managed the database and the administrative side of the business, and his good friend Willie Dawson served as vice president and pursued accounts with Alvin. Alvin worked at IBM from 7 A.M. to 3 P.M. Then he came home, grabbed something to eat, and got on the phone to drum up business. All three of them were working all of their waking hours, but Alvin had enough time left over to be nervous.

"Without a doubt, I was scared. Oh, my gosh!" Alvin remembers that this new venture into the unknown raised all of the usual questions: What if I'm not able to bring in enough money? What if I fail? What will people say about me? Alvin had fuel for the latter anxiety because people were already telling him, "Man, you're crazy," he reports. "Yeah, I was scared, but I knew if I stayed focused, it would work. I kept my eyes on the prize."

Alvin and Willie ran a serious collections campaign during the evenings, trying to persuade small businesses to contract them for services. In the beginning, their clients were mostly video stores, small doctor's offices, anyone who would give a new company some receivables. "We were able to build up a nice clientele," Alvin says. "And some of the video stores did a nice volume of business so we could make a certain amount of money and keep reinvesting it back into the business."

> *People were telling him, "Man, you're crazy," Alvin recalls. "Yeah, I was scared, but I knew if I stayed focused, it would work."*

They did not take a dime out of D & R for a year and, under that kind of management, the company blossomed, although it only earned about $12,000 the first year. Their timing in launching the business was lucky: in 1992, the economy started a phenomenal upswing. An explosive economy boosts consumer confidence, leading to increased spending, which in turn can lead to overspending and a cash shortfall when all the bills are due for payment. As a consequence, more companies are then looking for ways to collect outstanding debt and avoid delinquency without alienating debtors. This provided an opportunity for a small but innovative agency like D & R.

Tough Love

TO attract bigger clients, D & R has instituted a program called the Early Charge-Off Prevention Program (ECOP). Through ECOP,

D & R places a courtesy call to customers of clients, reminding the debtor that a charge or bill is outstanding and a service is about to be discontinued. Many companies that used to handle these calls in-house are outsourcing this function to collection agencies. The preemptive strike, or "pre-collect service," can save D & R clients up to forty percent in collection costs by avoiding the more expensive options of eating the loss or going after the debtor through legal channels.

In ECOP, D & R makes their money on a flat fee, unlike with traditional collections, which are calculated on a contingency or commission basis. The rate for each client is set based on how old the account is to be collected, how many accounts the client sends to D & R, and other factors. On an average, D& R is paid twenty-five percent of the amount collected through ECOP. The service is of mutual benefit to client and collector: serious cost savings for the client and serious money for D & R.

TCI Communications of Baltimore has experienced a twenty-two percent reduction in charge-offs due to ECOP. For another client, D & R has reduced their soft disconnects (accounts which are still active but in danger of being terminated for overdue payment) by forty percent. "What used to be $1 million a month in charge-offs is now $600,000," notes Alvin. "There are only a handful of companies that offer that kind of service."

Knowing bad credit can mess up a person's life, Alvin tries hard to work out a way for the debtor to pay the bill.

ECOP has become tremendously popular among present clients and is an attractive draw to potential ones. In fact, the demand has driven D & R debt recovery to devote much more time and effort to pre-collection. "A year ago we were ninety percent a traditional debt collection agency and ten percent outsourcing [ECOP]," Alvin says. "Now, we're fifty-fifty.

Our clients really love this program and we're in current discussions with AT&T, Bell Atlantic Mobile, and local utility companies."

According to the Cedar Grove, New Jersey–based Commercial Collection Agency Section (CCAS) of the Commercial Law League of America, the oldest creditor's rights organization in the country, getting rid of customer debt is of immense benefit to creditors because the likelihood that the money will be collected once an account goes into delinquent status diminishes significantly over time. After three months, the chances of collecting fall to about seventy percent, and they plummet to around twenty-eight percent after a year. Along with these statistics, overall consumer debt is increasing. In the United States in 1998, consumer debt totaled about $1.2 trillion dollars, nearly four percent more than for the previous year. Both consumer and commercial bankruptcies are also on the rise.

Although D & R makes money whether the debt gets paid or not, Alvin would rather help debtors than hurt them. Knowing bad credit can mess up a person's life, he tries hard during the collection process to work out a way for the debtor to pay the bill. He has discovered that most debtors really want to pay and get out of debt as quickly as possible. There are, according to Alvin, only a few people who refuse to pay their bills; most are unable to pay due to a family or medical crisis. With that in mind, the D & R collection process is based on a variation of the tough-love philosophy in an effort to help consumers find their own solutions.

The process begins with a survey, asking debtors a number of questions to determine the nature of the problem, and then moves to an attempt to get the consumer to commit to a payment schedule. D & R is willing to be flexible about time to a certain degree because, as Alvin states, it's not a race against the clock; the goal is to get the debt paid off.

If the debtor can't or won't commit to a payment schedule, the next step is to discuss other possibilities. "A lot of people don't realize they have options," says Alvin. "They can consolidate their debt by taking out a second mortgage or borrowing against an insurance policy or a 401(K) [retirement] plan. They can ask for a cash advance or borrow the money from family."

If all else fails, D & R goes back to its client to negotiate an acceptable partial payment to settle the account amicably and avoid legal action.

With its kinder, gentler approach, in 1998, D & R collected more than $4.2 million in debt, with revenues of just under $1 million.

With its kinder, gentler approach, in 1998, D & R collected more than $4.2 million in debt, with revenues of just under $1 million. Alvin projects that the company will experience a growth spurt to $240 million in collections in 1999. Since its inception in 1992, the company has grown over four hundred percent, an accomplishment of which Alvin is most proud.

Challenges and the Future

THERE have been, of course, obstacles along the way. The biggest difficulty, according to Alvin, has been to convince corporate America that a small minority business can do the same job as the big guys can. "There is a serious stigma attached that a small company or minority company just can't do the job," says Alvin. D & R has been able to overcome that prejudice, partly by offering a written guarantee of their performance. For example, if a client agrees to give D & R $1 million in overdue accounts and Alvin believes they can provide a twenty percent return based on their experience in the industry, he will put it in writing. If D & R falls short of that, it will pay the difference. "We haven't had to pay anyone any money," notes Alvin.

Like many young entrepreneurs, Alvin is motivated by the challenge, especially when people try to tell him he can't do something. "I always ask, what can we do to make that no a yes?" he says. "From my business to my personal life, there have been so many things I've been involved with where people said this is not going to happen. If you tell me that, I'll make sure it happens."

Whether racism has had an impact on business—landing it and keeping it—is a subject Alvin would prefer not to pursue. He tries hard not to read racism into a situation, personal or professional, preferring instead to give people the benefit of the doubt until he has run out of options. He has been this way since he was young. "I was always on the defensive, saying, 'Well, maybe they're just trying to make me tougher or more independent.' Even to this day, when I get that type of opposition, I'm always trying to turn it around and not make it a racist thing, even though I know it is," says Alvin. "My thing is if I give a man any type of power, or say I can't do this because of him or because of the white man, I'm never going to get it done."

On the other side of the equation, as a highly successful African American business, D & R is a role model and the object of acclaim. After the company was featured in *Black Enterprise,* Alvin reports receiving calls from all over the country from people who were inspired by his story. "To have people say, 'You know what? You've helped me with my perspective and helped me to understand that I can do this,' means a lot to me. It is gratifying to know that someone else is given hope because they've read or heard about D & R."

One woman called after the article ran and left a message, hoping for a sympathetic ear, but not believing that Alvin would ever call her back. When he did, she burst into tears and told him all her woes: for the first time since she had started her own business, she didn't think she could make payroll, her son was incarcerated, and her father was ill and getting sicker. When Alvin called her back, she had made payroll, had heard from her son for the first time in a long time, and had been able to get her father into a nursing home. The fact that Alvin called her back was icing on the cake.

"She said that when I called her back to tell her that everything was going to be all right, she was on the verge of quitting," recalls Alvin. "She told me, 'Just because you called me today, I am going to make sure that I keep pursuing.' That really rocked my world. It was really touching. I told her that hearing those words from her was one of the highlights of my career." Alvin and she still keep in touch.

Postscript

THE legacy Alvin Rice wants to leave is a simple one. He'd like to be remembered for his ability to make things happen. As his wife lovingly sums it up: "Whatever this guy believed in, he truly pursued and got it."

To Alvin, future prospects for entrepreneurs like himself are good. He believes that more African Americans are becoming aware of the economic possibilities and as a result are more interested in starting their own businesses. Alvin wonders aloud whether that may be a function of both time *and* place, whether part of the reason he stepped into the realm of entrepreneurship is because he lives in an area where there is a large, active black community to support black business and aspirations. "I don't know if it's being in Washington, D.C., but while I was in Columbus, I couldn't see it," he says, referring to the risky leap into business ownership. "I have friends my age living there who would say, 'I can't believe what you're doing.'"

The biggest difficulty has been to convince corporate America that a small minority business can do the same job as the big guys can.

Alvin understands that attitude, although he is clearly happy he does not share it. He is optimistically cautious about what lies ahead, meaning he appreciates his good fortune but takes nothing for granted regarding his future or that of the black community as a whole. "Even if I'm a millionaire, I'm never going to be naive enough to think that this cannot be taken from me," he says.

Although he would be sorry to lose it all, he does not measure his success by the size of his bank account. His personal idea of real failure is an inability to help someone who needs it, not to meet his family objectives, or not to realize his business ambitions. "I really want to hit the goals that I've set for this company," he says. "If I don't hit those, then that's failure to me."

CHAPTER

Class Act

Sibrena Stowe,
President and CEO
Stowe Communications, Inc.
Long Island, New York

Founded: 1997
1998 Revenues: $2.5 million
Number of Employees: 3
Initial Investment: $15,000
Current Net Worth: $3 million

S IBRENA STOWE ARRIVED in New York City in early 1997 with a child and $1,000, all the money she had in the world. She was a single mother without a job or prospects, armed only with intelligence, drive, and faith in her ability to do whatever she set out to accomplish.

Today, she is the president and CEO of Stowe Communications, Inc., a $3 million media-buying, advertising, and publicity company based on Long Island. Sibrena was drawn to the notoriously difficult and fickle entertainment business as a fly is drawn to honey. It was an attraction she could only deny so long before she felt compelled to leave her extended family and native suburban Philadelphia home to tackle New York.

Her road to riches has been marked by tragedy and other less traumatic but no less formidable stumbling blocks. A less determined woman might have retreated into the relative safety of a nine-to-five and a regular, if substantially smaller, paycheck. But Sibrena is a striver and a die-hard believer that ownership is the key to freedom. And she states matter-of-factly, "I can't work for other people."

It is true that she would not fit easily into the typical corporate environment. For one thing, everything that crosses her mind is mirrored in her face. In case you miss that unspoken message, she will clarify it for you by telling you exactly what she thinks. And she has no problem with being known as brutally frank.

Stowe Communications, with $2.5 million in revenues in 1998, does everything from tactical planning for television and radio spot buys to special events planning. Sibrena also writes a feature page in *Inner City* magazine called "Class Act," which gives artists advice about how to evolve and grow professionally.

Going After What She Wants

AT thirty, Sibrena is young for the position she fills, but she has mastered the field of media buying (the strategic purchase of advertising space and time for clients who want to reach a particular audience, expand their market, or increase name recognition) and comprehends the advertising/media environment, consumer desires, and client needs with the depth and breadth of one with twice her experience. When it comes to business and life, Sibrena is unstoppable. An anecdote is illustrative of her style.

In 1995, Sibrena happened to be at city hall in Philadelphia, where President Clinton was scheduled to stop on a routine reelection junket. She was not on the Secret Service list of approved guests but wanted to meet the president, so she had a politically connected family friend make a phone call and soon found herself shaking hands with Bill Clinton. The first words out of her mouth?

"You need me."

Bill Clinton: "For what?"

Sibrena, in a tone that suggested he should know this already: "To be your assistant press secretary."

> *A less determined woman might have retreated into the relative safety of a nine-to-five and a regular, if substantially smaller, paycheck.*

He smiled at her bravado and said, "Send your résumé to Dee Dee Myers," referring to his press secretary at the time. The news cameras caught her for the first evening broadcast, smiling and shaking the hand of the president, the only one in red among the conservatively dressed, blue-suited throng. She never sent her résumé to Dee Dee Myers, but she had made an impression on the most powerful man in the free world.

With a combination of charm, a little flattery, and an iron-fisted will, she has almost single-handedly built a successful business and commands the respect of her corporate and individual clients, which include, among a host of others, Universal Records, Kedar Entertainment, Iron Mike Entertainment, singer Erykah Badu, and rapper Rakim. And she has done it in a little less than two years while being an on-duty, full-time mom to daughter, Natasha, now eleven. Sibrena Stowe is an inspiration to every would-be entrepreneur who has dreamed of breaking out of the rut and away from the pack to live and work on his or her own terms.

Groomed for the Spotlight

BY the time Sibrena was five years old, she was a seasoned performer. Three days a week, she rode the bus from suburban Montgomery County into Philadelphia to attend acting, ballet, tap, and jazz dance classes at the renowned Philadelphia Freedom Theater, the oldest African American dance theater in the country. Sibrena also sang in the choir and played the piano and flute. She idolized dancer Debbie Allen (future choreographer for multiple Academy Award shows) and planned to become a dancer like her. Sibrena had family in the Bronx and spent happy summers there, away from the strict discipline of home. She daydreamed about moving to New York City to study ballet at the American Ballet Theater. "New York was my mother's dream," says Sibrena, "and it rubbed off on me."

As she grew older, Sibrena recognized that she was much shorter and more shapely than most prima ballerinas. While that dream faded, she never stopped loving the spotlight and performed often, most memorably as Rizzo in her high school's production of *Grease*. School held her interest less than performing. A self-described rebellious teen, Sibrena had ideas of her own early on. Although her mother was big on education, what Sibrena liked best about her upper-class school in suburban Landsdale, Pennsylvania, was the freedom to pick her own classes. Those that grabbed her attention were economics, communications, and Spanish. She loved to write and she read constantly, both because her mother insisted on her participation in reading programs and because she is a lover of books and a seeker of knowledge.

When it came to material possessions, she had everything a child could want. Although her parents divorced when she was fifteen and her mother remarried, Sibrena the teenager had clothes, a car, and money. But her mother, an oncology nurse, bartender, and member of the army reserve, was also a strict disciplinarian who believed in teaching her daughter the value of independence and responsibility, both by example and decree. Sibrena routinely did chores and did not date until she was seventeen, although she laughingly remembers one boy who would come and sit on her steps, lovelorn and ignored, until her mother would ask, "Doesn't he have a home?"

All of this was fine with Sibrena until she turned eighteen and fell in love for the first time. The man who would become her daughter's father was a handsome, slightly reckless young man who swept her off her feet and made her lose her mind. One week after her eighteenth birthday, she sneaked out

> *With a combination of charm, a little flattery, and an iron-fisted will, Sibrena has almost single-handedly built a successful business.*

of her mother's house in the middle of the night and moved in with him. She speaks of her abrupt exit with regret. "She [my mother] woke up one morning and I was gone."

Sibrena left high school shortly before graduation and soon became pregnant, which her mother knew upon seeing her even though Sibrena was far from showing. Her mother could have been angry, but surprisingly she was not, instead welcoming the prospect of her first grandchild.

Sibrena, who had rebelled against some of the strictures her mother imposed but learned her lessons well, got a high school equivalency diploma and began scouting around for careers. The field of journalism pulled her, but her mother advocated for practical knowledge, encouraging her to find something solid to fall back on "because journalists don't make any money." Sibrena settled on paramedic classes and attended a program at Hahnemann University in Philadelphia to obtain her certificate.

Certificate in hand, Sibrena could not find a paramedic job in Philadelphia, so she tried a change of scene by moving to Florida, where her mother's family originated. By this time, Natasha was five and lived with her father half the year and Sibrena the other half. Still unable to find a paramedic job, Sibrena answered a classified ad promising up to $400 a week, which led her to a job in Jacksonville as a marketer for a closed-circuit television security and surveillance company. There, an innocuous company routine changed her life.

Every morning, before it was time to meet potential customers, the marketers listened to inspirational tapes by famous motivational speakers such as Les Brown and Tony Robbins. Sibrena was riveted by the messages about self-esteem, selling, and making money and listened to the tapes on off hours, even in her car on the way to the office. The messages lit a dormant fire in Sibrena to strike out on her own. Before she could formulate a plan, tragedy struck.

Loss and a New Start

IN February 1993, when she had been in Florida for two years, she got a call from one of her mother's eight sisters to come home—her mother was in the hospital. Upon arriving in Philadelphia, she didn't even drop off her bags but went immediately to the University of Pennsylvania hospital, where she learned that her mother was suffering from breast cancer that had metastasized to her lungs. Sibrena quit her job in Florida on the spot and set about taking care of her mom—helping her get into the tub, cooking her meals, and generally making her last days on earth as comfortable as possible. Five months later, her mother had a stroke, and a month after that she died, with Sibrena by her side.

Heartbroken but resolute, Sibrena moved in with her mother's sister Tia and began to look for a job. Money had become a problem in the months between quitting her job and her mother's death, but she found that she was ineligible even for temporary assistance such as food stamps because she had voluntarily left her job in Florida and was no longer a Pennsylvania resident. Sibrena had to take the first job that came along and, amazingly, that happened to be a scout for a talent agency.

The job required extensive travel and, on one trip, calling to check on Natasha at her father's house as usual, she got no answer for two consecutive days. Panicked, she returned to Philadelphia, to find more trouble. Natasha's paternal grandmother was sick in the hospital and Natasha had been left with neighbors during the crisis. Finding this completely unacceptable, Sibrena again quit her job and began looking for something close to home so that she could be certain Natasha had a stable home environment.

A succession of seemingly unrelated jobs and pursuits ensued. She worked in public relations at the YMCA and in advertising for Montgomery Publishing. She attended classes in communications at Montgomery County Community College. She interned in the public affairs department at Philadelphia's popular Power 99 radio and worked in the advertising department as well, which laid the foundation for her to approach music companies with confidence when she started Stowe Communications. At the radio station, she did not see eye to eye with her boss, chafed under imposed rules of corporate conduct, and resented the inevitable politics of organizational interaction. The experience brought to a head her dissatisfaction with working for others and not making much money in the process.

Sibrena realized she couldn't keep working for $7 an hour and sacrificing her personality. She knew she had to create her own wealth.

Sibrena realized she couldn't keep working for $7 an hour and sacrificing her personality. "I understand role playing, but I can't do it consistently," she says. "I knew I had to create my own wealth." She thought back to the motivational lessons she had learned as a marketer in

Florida, to the books she had read by Napoleon Hill and Tony Robbins, and thought, "I want to take those lessons and apply them to my life."

A recent four-month stint as a temp at Dean Witter investment brokerage had not only taught her about investing and the stock market, but whetted her appetite for more of everything—more money, more control over her life. She began to study successful people and thought the best way to become one of them was to mirror their actions. She also still hungered for New York, so in January of 1997 she went there, put a deposit on an apartment, and, with Natasha in tow, left Philadelphia behind.

New York State of Mind

SIBRENA ended up back in the Bronx at an apartment that rented for $700 a month. Besides her $1,000, there was some money coming from the sale of a house her mother had willed to her and child support, which all went to Natasha. That was it. Since living in New York is not cheap, Sibrena's first order of business was to find a job. She again turned to the classified ads and found a position as an independent contractor in advertising sales with Gelwicks Agency, New York's oldest advertising firm. She was soon making five sales a week, an unusual success rate, and bringing in a volume of new business. Things were looking up until, once again, trouble struck.

In May, Sibrena was hit by a car near her apartment, receiving an injury that put her in a toe-to-thigh cast and confined her to home for two months. Fortunately, an insurance settlement from a previous injury came through, so she had two months to think about what she really wanted to do. She began with what she knew how to do.

Her experience at Power 99 had given her confidence that she understood music and what audiences want and, of course, she knew advertising like the back of her hand. She had a friend introduce her to Aariane Pope, who was the assistant to Kojo Bentil, vice president of Kedar Entertainment. Through Aariane, she convinced Kojo to let her do a marketing plan for print, radio, broadcast, and cable television media buys for Kedar clients Erykah Badu and Rakim.

The way media buying works is that the person doing the buying on a client's behalf gets a percentage of the time she bought. What Sibrena found is that print media give music labels a built-in discount on the fee, so there was no reason to hire Sibrena to manage advertising if they were already paying less for previously contracted services. However, no such arrangement existed in television and radio. That was where she found a gap in services and her niche. The plan she revised for Kedar focused on broadcast and cable. They liked her ideas and she got the contract. She pitched Universal Records at the same time and got that contract as well.

> "*E*very person I have asked if I could handle their public relations has either said yes or no. The ones who said no have come back to me."

How did she find clients? "I asked them," she says, laughing, proving yet again that sometimes it takes simple assertiveness to reach a goal. "Every person I have asked if I could handle their public relations has either said yes or no. The ones who said no have come back to me."

As a young African American woman, she had some instinctive knowledge about how to advertise artists such as Erykah Badu and Rakim. Traditional ad agencies without an understanding of the urban market, especially as regards the new crop of hip-hop artists, would make fatal ad buy mistakes. For example, you don't buy advertising time on *Seinfeld* for a gangsta rapper—it's an audience/advertising mismatch. Instead, you buy time on a show such as the black comedy stand-up series *Def Jam*.

More specific to Sibrena's experience, when she bought time for rapper D. J. Quik, who is big on the West Coast and in the Southwest, she had to do a plan for his company, Arista, that focused on the East Coast and targeted the appropriate outlets. Arista's roster of talent includes more mainstream artists such as Whitney Houston. When Arista started signing rappers, it became necessary to hire people like Sibrena, who know the rap world and market. "Growing up in the hip-hop generation, I understand the artists, I understand the demographics, and I understand the market," says Sibrena.

Where she lacked understanding, she turned to mentors for help, calling on former bosses and even her high school communications teacher for advice. For financing to start the business, she used $15,000, the inheritance that finally arrived, and she asked her boss, Frank Coe, a partner at Gelwicks, to back her. With his support, she got important outlets like MTV and The Box to front her credit for ad buys and she was in business in September 1997 as Stowe Communications. With Kedar and Universal onboard, she was able to total $1.5 million in advertising sales in just three months.

A Day in the Life

IN addition to public relations and publicity for entertainers and sports figures, Stowe Communications, with a grand total of three employees, also does special events planning. On a recent day, Sibrena was on the phone trying to figure out how to organize participants in New York's West Indian Day Parade, the largest event of its kind for people of Caribbean descent. It seems that rap magnate Sean "Puffy" Combs and bad girl rapper Lil' Kim could not share a float because they are on different record labels. Between calls to Mike Tyson's agency, D. J. Scratch (a client whose premiere she was attending that night), and rapper Charli Baltimore's agent ("You should just let me represent Charli, you ain't doin' nothin' with her."), she telephoned a friend's house to make sure Natasha had eaten and would be home soon.

Typically, Sibrena books a heavy schedule of longer days Monday through Wednesday to deal with local and West Coast clients but tries to keep Thursday and Friday light to spend time with Natasha.

Sibrena slides easily between personalities: she can be the well-bred upper-class Philadelphian or a homegirl, depending on who is on the other end of the line. While dealing with the daily details of running a business, she keeps her mind on the long term and speculates out loud about the market and key investments she has made, which are paying off handsomely as the economy rides a record wave of high returns.

She is a deft negotiator, believes in asking for what she wants, up front, no games, and is a no-nonsense businesswoman—especially when it comes to getting paid. She collects on time, for the most part, because she demands it, even from some of the biggest names in the bad attitude, shoot-you-as-soon-as-look-at-you world of gangsta rappers. Sibrena is clear that she brooks no back talk and that Stowe does not advance credit.

"I tell them that there's only one God. I worship him, and everybody else should just pay me my money," she says, laughing. She is indeed a devout Catholic who attends mass every Sunday, but the other six days of the week are devoted to some strategic thought or action about business and where she is going next. As a woman who wants to retire at thirty-five, she is busily making sure that her money, her business, and her investments work for her. (She plans to make strategic investments in real estate as a way to diversify her portfolio.)

> *Sibrena slides easily between personalities: she can be the well-bred upper-class Philadelphian or a homegirl, depending on who's on the other end of the line.*

As for the future of Stowe Communications, Sibrena would like to see the company push the boundaries within the field of media buying to include new and diverse accounts such as movie distributors, production houses, and rock bands because she feels she can bring the same insight to their advertising strategy that she has brought to hip-hop artists. She cites, for example, last year's *Hav Plenty,* a critically acclaimed black comedy that flopped at the box office partially because, according to Sibrena, the marketing strategy was all wrong.

"I talked to Miramax, but they hired another firm that wasn't familiar with the intended demographic and the advertisements were not optimally placed," declares Sibrena. "I want people to know that they should stipulate in their contracts who they want to market their film. If they don't, the film can flop because of poor marketing. *Hav Plenty* is a perfect example." Her analysis is right on, according to film producers, black authors, and others who have said for years that it takes a different approach to market black products.

> *"I believe what goes around comes around. It's important to be loyal to your clients; they have to be able to trust you."*

Professionally, Sibrena dreams of producing feature films, television projects, and documentaries. Personally, she hopes to marry and have more children. She has been close to marriage a few times but, she maintains, "it takes a strong man to be with me."

Although she has entrée to the parties and lifestyle most people only read about in *Vanity Fair,* Sibrena likes simple pleasures: going to the library, walking on the nearby beach, hanging out with her daughter. Her interactions with Natasha make it clear that she means it when she says she is family oriented, which also demonstrated by the close relationship she maintains with her extended family back in suburban Philadelphia, especially her grandmother, with whom she has a standing phone date every Sunday. Of her move away from them, she says, "I've always wanted to live here [in New York], even though I didn't want to leave my family. I have to go where the money is."

Family has been both her support and her springboard to success. "All of my cousins are successful; they are all doing positive things," says Sibrena, adding that most are involved in Philadelphia politics, the equivalent of the "family business" if there is one and something for which she had little patience.

Rather than serve the community through politics, she gives in a more personal way. "My plan to give back to the black community is to lead by example," she says. That is her philosophy at work and at home. She takes Natasha to work with her so that her daughter can see what she does during the day. She explains the market to Natasha and the logic of buying and selling stock to give her a head start on understanding the world of business. Natasha was deemed a genius in second grade and has been reading the newspaper since she was four because Mommy did it.

Sibrena's business philosophy is based on loyalty and trust. "I believe what goes around comes around," she says. "It's important to be loyal to your clients; they have to be able to trust you. And I try to please them because word of mouth is what helped me grow."

And Sibrena Stowe makes it clear that her growing is far from over. Stowe Communications is not the final act for Sibrena. "I have a destiny. This is not the most I'm going to do," she says. "My drive is life."

CHAPTER

Up and Comers: People to Watch

Debbie Kirkland
Claranai Records and Starfire Entertainment, Inc.

Kimberly Lee Minor
MLS Collections, Ltd.

Steven D. White
S. D. White & Associates, Inc.

Kelly Peterson and Aboubacar Sissoko
AMS Consulting, Inc.

John Logan
Logan Transfer Company

All Show and Substance

Debbie Kirkland
President and CEO
Claranai Records and Starfire Entertainment, Inc.
Silver Spring, Maryland

Founded: 1993 (Starfire), 1998 (Claranai)
1998 Revenues: $250,000
Number of Employees: 1
Initial Investment: $36,000 (Starfire),
$100,000 (Claranai)
Current Net Worth: $600,000

Debbie Kirkland always dreamed of being a recording artist. Not one to wait around for the fates to decide her destiny, she founded a record label, cut a CD, and has taken to the road to promote her debut, *Debbie Kirkland, In Session.* Best characterized as a jazz fusion hybrid, *In Session* incorporates a wide range of influences, from traditional jazz and Brazilian to pop and funk. Debbie—whose sound has been compared to that of Nancy Wilson and Eloise Laws—is garnering critical acclaim, with reviewers of the CD rapturously declaring it "poetic," "alluring," and "sensual."

The CD's first single, "Who," is now in heavy rotation on some of the largest urban adult/contemporary stations in the country, playing from California to Washington, D.C., Texas to New York, and most points in between. She recently discovered that she is being played in London as well, a pleasant surprise. The rapidly growing success of the CD means that her label, Claranai Records, has definitely hit the ground running.

The Substance Behind the Show

DEBBIE Kirkland has her act together—on *and* off the stage. The woman who has performed with some of the greatest names in music, including George Duke, Lonny Liston Smith, and Sonny Stitt, to name a few, is also the president and CEO of Starfire Entertainment, Inc., a talent management agency based in Silver Spring, Maryland. Starfire manages over sixty acts and bands, solo guitarists, singers, string quartets, and other musicians. Together, Starfire and Claranai are worth an estimated $600,000.

Debbie, thirty-seven, is something of an anomaly in a business in which stories of famous and fabulously wealthy performers who were mismanaged into poverty are so common as to be cliché. But Debbie has absolutely no intention of

> "*I* started Claranai Records because I didn't want to give control to a label that might take me where I don't want to go."

ending up as that kind of tragic footnote in music history. A talented singer onstage, she is a shrewd and savvy businesswoman behind the scenes. And both the management company and the record label are owned solely by Debbie Kirkland. Running two businesses and performing on top of that has been bone-wearying work, and she has paid some heavy dues, but Debbie wouldn't have it any other way.

"I started Claranai because no one is responsible for paying for my dream but me," says Debbie. "And I didn't want to give up control to sign with a label that might take me where I don't want to go. So I created my own thing."

Beautiful and brainy, Debbie, who claims she was "born singing," traveled around the world performing and tried a couple of other nonstarter careers before she finally settled in her hometown of Washington, D.C. Throughout high school, her University of Maryland college years, and her twenties, she sang everywhere—from street corners to exclusive clubs—and performed with a number of local area bands. She finally landed with a talent management company, which took a substantial cut of performance profits. Even so, they fired her in 1993 after seven years because the company thought *she* was making too much money. Debbie took it as a sign and simultaneously created her own band-for-hire, *Starfire,* and the talent agency of the same name.

Her versatility and wide-ranging knowledge of musical styles— from Jewish klezmer music to Motown to country and western— made her bread-and-butter band a wildly successful local act with constant bookings for weddings, bar mitzvahs, corporate parties, and country clubs, among other venues. Those engagements allowed her to expand her network to encompass a variety of musicians who were as impressed with her ability to manage the business of her band as they were with her voice.

Debbie soon took on the management of those performers and musicians, building Starfire Entertainment into a respected and successful enterprise with an impressive roster of musical talent. The company, in turn, helped bankroll the creation of Claranai in early 1997. All her endeavors are self-financed from a combination of savings and investment earnings. Of course, the money she earns goes back into the businesses. As for Starfire, the band, she still performs with them when she is not on tour.

Named for her mother, Clara Harris, and her grandmother, whom she called "Nay-Nay," Claranai Records is the fulfillment of Debbie Kirkland's greatest wish, a first step toward stardom but, more important, a giant leap toward artistic freedom and the autonomy to make her own business decisions. Debbie's philosophy is that you make your own luck, especially in the entertainment world. "You know, I've met a number of people who can help me, and that's nice," says Debbie matter-of-factly. "But I can't wait around with my hand out, saying 'please.'" She brings the same no-nonsense, get-it-done attitude to everything from how her image is crafted to how the books are handled, overseeing all of it with input from a tight circle of advisors.

Along with her two business endeavors, Debbie, who is married and has two young daughters, puts family high on her long list of priorities. In the middle of a recent promotional junket, she flew home to see the girls off on their first day of summer camp and did the same in a fit of whimsy to celebrate the second birthday of her dog, Beta.

On her sojourns back from the road, she makes sure that Starfire is running as smoothly as the family, and then she takes off again to introduce the world to a woman who can produce the silkiest sounds this side of Cassandra Wilson, all the while plotting the rise of Claranai and the possibility of signing other talent to her label. Debbie Kirkland is juggling it all and has not dropped a single ball yet. If her will holds, and there is no reason to believe it won't, success is all but guaranteed for this star on the rise.

Cornering the Market on Style

Kimberly Lee Minor
President and CEO
MSL Collections, Ltd.
Columbus, Ohio

Founded: 1998
1998 Revenues: $75,000
Number of Employees: 1
Initial Investment: $75,000
Current Net Worth: $100,000

The sartorial ghettoization of large-size women is over, and they can thank Kimberly Lee Minor that they are free at last. Kim, thirty-five, is the president and CEO of MSL Collections, Ltd., the first company to produce haute-fashion career, casual, and special occasion wear for women sized 4 through 28W. In an industry typically geared to sizes 2 through 14, MSL is as refreshing as a drink of cool water to a parched tongue.

The sophisticated line, which is evocative of Donna Karan and Ellen Tracy, is distinguished by its use of luxurious fabrics to enhance quality and provide subtle shaping for every size. The line has received praise from fashion critics, garnered a coterie of loyal fans, and gained the attention of such premier outlets as Nordstrom and Federated Department Stores, owners of Macy's.

Kim was formerly a senior buyer for Macy's, Limited, and Express (the number one specialty retailer for women's clothes in the country). Her objective in creating a clothing line, she explains, was to rewrite the book of style for all women, including the often overlooked, undervalued real-life, full-size woman. It was a niche market desperately in need of a quality product. "I am focused on providing a look for women so they feel like women, not a dress size," says Kim, who is fashion-model beautiful but all business. "My goal is to make it a pleasure for women to shop and dress and to ensure that the woman who wears a larger size looks good even if she doesn't wear what is considered an 'average' size."

Her parallel goal was to free herself from working for other people. With an original investment from savings of $75,000, Kim launched MSL in 1998 before a capacity crowd at the trendy New York City Sugar Bar. It was clear that Kim had struck gold. Women and men responded with wild enthusiasm to the clothes, and the line was featured in *MODE, Belle,* and *Woman's Day* magazines. MSL clothing is currently carried in select boutiques in New York and the Midwest, and the company was recently approached by Black Entertainment Television to possibly dress some of its on-air talent.

Making a Name

THE struggle to succeed is not over. The fashion business is one of the most competitive industries and, like other designer lines that were young once (such as FUBU and Karl Kani, Inc.), the company has an uphill battle ahead. To break from the ranks of competitors and become a recognizable brand is the goal, and it takes persistence to be heard over the din of voices vying for attention in the fashion field. The struggle is to maintain a solid company while the clothing line comes to the attention of more big-name buyers and, of course, the public.

MSL, which is based in Columbus, Ohio, broke even its first year, and Kim expects that the company will do well if certain objectives are reached. For one, the company needs an infusion of capital while it builds its name and establishes an identity. So she needs to devote

> *"I am focused on providing a look for women so they feel like women, not a dress size."*

equal time to raising money and raising awareness about the brand, which is really a job for two people. Columbus is not a fashion hub—although it is the world headquarters for the Limited and Express—and that has caused some problems in terms of visibility and logistics, such as getting patterns, samples, and fabrics at a reasonable price and in a timely manner.

"Most clothing businesses take at least five years, if not longer, to become established," says Kim. "What's important to remember is that you haven't failed until you say you can't do it."

She has no intention of giving in that easily. An entrepreneur since the seventh grade—she catered parties for her mother's friends—Kim had an artistic bent as well as the desire to run her own company. Between graduating from Temple University with a degree in radio, television, and film and entrance into the MBA program at Drexel University, the Philadelphia-area native ran her own talent management agency. She ended up dropping out of Drexel when she made a decision to put her money and energy into KRL (Kimberly Rae Lee) Management full time.

That enterprise did not pan out and, in 1986, Kim entered Macy's management training program. There she met the woman who would become her mentor, Andrea Blake. Kim had designed and made all of her own gowns for prom and other events but had never ventured to do so professionally. Andrea encouraged her to develop her eye and nurtured her innovative take on design. When Andrea left Macy's, Kim stepped into her place and became the buyer for the young men's collection. Kim was wooed away soon after by Express in Columbus. She made it clear that as a quid pro quo for relocating to Ohio, she wanted to learn the business. She became the first person in the company to jump from planning and allocation to merchandising. After a few years at Express, during which she became a senior buyer and managed a division that brought in $350 million in sales, she felt ready to take the ultimate risk.

As Kim develops MSL, she maintains two lucrative side businesses: one, managing special events where she can showcase MSL designs and two, a stage and set design business under the rubric of Sepia Productions, Inc. These businesses bring in some income and are also flexible enough to afford her time to build the clothing company. Although it was obviously risky, she knows that she did the right thing by seeking her independence. While growing up, Kim says, she watched her parents struggle, not to make ends meet, but to be happy.

"My parents came from the mindset that when you find a job, you keep it forever and you're focused on making money and paying bills, not necessarily personal fulfillment," says Kim. "I want to be fulfilled and to own the golden egg." MSL may be a difficult undertaking, but it may also be her golden egg. "I want to do this for myself," says Kim, recalling that her mother was a big factor in the decision.

Before Marion Sanders Lee lost her battle with cancer in 1997, she encouraged her daughter to pursue her ambition of creating a fashion line. It was the final impetus Kim needed. "If I learned anything from my mother's passing, it is that tomorrow is not promised," says Kim. "It was now or never."

MSL, which bears her mother's initials, is a fitting tribute to a woman who was herself a pioneer, as one of the first African American models in Philadelphia. Now her daughter is fulfilling her fondest wish as she remains true to the memory of her mother and to herself.

From Nonprofit to For-Profit

Steven D. White
President and CEO
S. D. White & Associates, Inc.
Beltsville, Maryland

Founded: 1997
1998 Revenues: $130,000
Number of Employees: 2, plus 85 associates
Initial Investment: $10,000
Current Net Worth: $250,000

Contrary to popular belief, nonprofit does not necessarily mean no money—at least not for thirty-five-year-old Steven D. White. Steven founded S. D. White & Associates, Inc. (SDW&A), an organizational development and management consulting firm, in March of 1997. With an original investment of $10,000 and a dozen years of business and nonprofit, political, and local government management experience, the president and CEO of the new firm feels it was the best investment he could have made with the money from his savings and retirement plan.

"I was tired of hearing leaders of nonprofit organizations saying they couldn't find qualified people of color to perform important managerial functions," says Steven. "I knew that wasn't true. You can't tell me the skill and talent don't exist in our community." Steven knows he is just one example of the type of talent out there creating innovative solutions for the management problems of the new millennium. "I started SDW&A for three basic reasons: (1) to showcase the skill and experience of dozens of people of color I know, (2) to offer consulting and systems-building support to progressive organizations throughout the United States and abroad, and (3) to earn a suitable living to support my wife and our two children."

> *"I was tired of hearing leaders of nonprofit organizations saying they couldn't find qualified people of color to perform important managerial functions."*

Steven expects it to take a lot of hard work to achieve his long-term goal of making S. D. White & Associates the largest organizational development and management consulting firm in the United States owned by people of color. Hard work is nothing new to Steven, and the proof is in his track record.

When he was twenty-five, he ran the successful campaign of John C. Daniels, the first black mayor of New Haven, Connecticut, raising over $400,000 in campaign funds, a record for a municipal campaign in the state of Connecticut. After the historic campaign in 1989, Steven went on to become the youngest member of the mayor's cabinet, serving the city of New Haven as legislative liaison. In December 1991, after helping Mayor Daniels secure a second term in office, he joined Marian Wright Edelman at the Children's Defense Fund and helped establish and raise millions for the Black Student Leadership Network and the Freedom Schools. These programs were designed to encourage and train black college students to become child advocates while providing community service work for children and families.

Steven has managed nearly every aspect of elections and nonprofit organizations, from the complex construction of a campaign platform and the substantive analysis of program development to the tedious task of campaign finance reporting and the arduous art of supervising an annual audit.

A Fluid Consortium

WITH projected revenues of $200,000 in 1999, SDW&A works with a fluid consortium of eighty-five professionals, academics, organizers, and trainers who are engaged on a project-by-project basis. National nonprofit organizations, small businesses, and government agencies in need of organizational development or services related to management can call on SDW&A for a solution tailored to meet their requirements. The services available include fund raising, event management, policy analysis, strategic planning, research and report generation, and technological advice.

Steven and his staff develop teams of professionals best suited for each project, allowing SDW&A to deliver the highest-quality service at a fraction of the cost of hiring full-time employees. Satisfied clients have included Amnesty International, the Center for Policy Alternatives, the Family Place, and the Leadership Center at Morehouse College.

SDW&A does ongoing, long-term work as well as one-time consultations. For example, for the past two and a half years, it administered and marketed the national portable pension plan for members of the National Organizers Alliance, a group that supports the social justice movement. Recently, SDW&A completed a Fund Feasibility Study for the National Center for Strategic Nonprofit Planning and Community Leadership, a Ford Foundation grantee working to develop the capacity of community-based organizations.

A consistent goal of SDW&A is to educate and empower clients while increasing organizational capacity to meet their needs internally. This is one reason for the company's client-tailored approach, which includes a training component when possible.

Steven plans to expand to a larger arena in the future. "First, we must play to our strength, and that is in the nonprofit sector," says

Steven. "But as we grow, we'll provide more service to for-profit corporations, starting with their community service and philanthropic arms, where they need to buttress their efforts." Strategically located in Beltsville, Maryland, between Baltimore and Washington, D.C., the company is situated along a corridor of the East Coast where there are arguably more powerful nonprofit organizations, government agencies, and for-profit corporations per square mile than in any other area of the country.

With its unique mix of program, policy, and business skills, SDW&A is thriving in the political and social issues world of Washington, D.C. Most of Washington is shopping a point of view that they would like to see become public policy in some form, and companies and agencies need internal systems and a solid financial base to better position themselves to be heard. SDW&A can help make that happen.

Raising money, a specialty of SDW&A, can be a lucrative enterprise. But Steven is less interested in making money and more interested in providing young people of color an alternative model for championing progressive ideas while earning a good living, which is one of the values he learned from his parents. To this day, these values prompt him to volunteer some services where he perceives the need is greatest. His company is proof that it is indeed possible to do well by doing good.

Global and Domestic Partners

AMS Consulting, Inc.
Kelly Peterson
President of Domestic Consulting Practice
Aboubacar Sissoko
President of International Consulting
Los Angeles, California

Founded: 1997
1998 Revenues: $200,000
Number of Employees: 2
Initial Investment: $30,000
Current Net Worth: $500,000

Going global is one of the fastest ways for a previously domestic operation to explore unplumbed business opportunities. That does not come as news to the husband-and-wife team who head up AMS Consulting, the umbrella corporation for Domestic Consulting Practice and International Consulting. Kelly Peterson and Aboubacar Sissoko each preside over their own division of the Los Angeles–based consulting company they founded in January 1997. Senegal-born Aboubacar is president of the international business and product development side, and Kelly is president of individual and corporate performance consulting in her native United States.

AMS bills itself as a company committed to offering the highest level of services in the dual areas of market development in Africa and domestic organizational and individual consulting. Kelly and Aboubacar have carved out specialties suited to their different areas of expertise and managed to make it work as partners at the office as well as at home.

A Growing Market

ON the international side, Aboubacar, known to his friends as "Backs," offers clients an objective third-party viewpoint on strategic planning, marketing, and other operational issues with a focus on Europe as well as developing democracies and markets in Africa and the Middle East. Backs, forty-three, who has lived in Europe, the United States, and his native Senegal, as well as other parts of Africa, uses his considerable knowledge of his home continent to bridge the yawning cultural gap between U.S. corporations and emerging African markets made up of people experiencing their first taste of life as global consumers.

An attorney, Backs received his J.D. from the University of Brussels, Belgium, with a specialty in maritime, space, and aviation transportation law, and master's degrees in both political science and international relations from the same university. With such expertise, he takes a more active role, when warranted, as an intermediary, guide, and advisor to corporations seeking to stimulate or penetrate markets in three key areas: services, such as telecommunications and transportation; pharmaceuticals, including equipment and medication; and consumer products, covering the gamut from sugar substitutes to refined oil.

The time to explore new possibilities is now, according to Backs, as former colonies stretch their wings as fledgling democracies. "As Africa moves away from its dependence on Europe, it is privatizing much of what were once government-run industries, like utilities," he says. "So the opportunities for market expansion are growing exponentially." Greater exposure to what's for sale in the world is also helping to generate demand across Africa. "All across Africa they have CNN, so they have more knowledge of the American market."

Backs helps that aspect of the business along by nurturing interest in American goods and products he represents, thus creating leads for market development. He also facilitates political and government relations for client companies and identifies possible financing partnerships.

Prior to starting AMS, Backs worked as a lawyer and consultant for various firms. He was recently nominated by the United Nations to be one of eight international ambassadors, heading American participation in the Goree Memorial Project. The project is the first international monument to slaves who passed through Goree Island, Senegal, which was used as a central port for the transatlantic slave trade. Among his duties, he is charged with raising $25 million for the project. In his spare time (of which there is little), Backs is an artist gaining a reputation in art circles and enjoying a measure of commercial success.

> *"As Africa moves away from its dependence on Europe, . . . the opportunities for market expansion are growing exponentially."*

Across the Atlantic

BACK on the domestic front, Kelly Peterson targets U.S. companies with an aggressive commitment to enhancing skill and performance development for employees. The industries she works with include retail and sales, entertainment, and small entrepreneurial technical companies.

With fifteen years of experience in human resources, sales, and training development, she helps companies analyze existing organizational functions, operations, and results and then recommends specific areas and actions for improvement. If corporations are interested in establishing in-house training programs, she helps design and implement programs and develops systems to evaluate them. Where outdated programs already exist, Kelly advises on how to redesign and update them.

She is currently working with the Walt Disney Company, facilitating a five-day management development program for mid- to senior-level executives identified for further advancement within the Disney organization. One of the premier management and training consultants in the country, Kelly, thirty-eight, was one of four consultants chosen in a nationwide search for facilitators to lead the Disney effort.

Kelly has bachelor of arts degrees in communications and social science and behavior from California State University at Northridge and is a certified master trainer with certificates from the University of California at Los Angeles and the University of Southern California. Before starting her own business, she was employed in the human resources department of Sony Pictures Entertainment for seven years. During this time she designed and implemented a management development training program, among other employee service functions. This gave her invaluable experience for her entrepreneurial venture.

> *Kelly was one of four consultants chosen in a nationwide search for facilitators to lead a Disney management development program.*

Kelly much prefers the life of an independent consultant. "I realized a while ago that corporate America was not for me," says Kelly. "But I had a desire to do professional development work with individuals. This is the perfect balance for me." Her work is no less demanding now that she is self-employed. A workaholic, she has facilitated over 100 sales training, motivation, and sales coaching seminars for Pacific Bell service representatives, conducted customer service and sales training for Universal Studios, and run team building for the Salvation Army. Despite her workaholism, Kelly still manages to find time to pursue her other loves: writing fiction and poetry.

Kelly and Backs started AMS Consulting with a $30,000 investment from Kelly's retirement plan. Now, in their third full year of operation, they predict revenues of $250,000, evidence that looking beyond geographic boundaries for business opportunities is an option worth exploring for entrepreneurs with an open mind.

Moving On Up

John Logan
President and CEO
Logan Transfer Company
Silver Spring, Maryland

Founded: 1985
1998 Revenues: $500,000
Number of Employees: 10 salaried employees
and 20–30 contract workers
Initial Investment: $0
Current Net Worth: $750,000

John Logan has taken the one thing most people hate to do—move—and made it pay. The Silver Spring, Maryland–based Logan Transfer Company is a commercial moving business devoted to large-scale office and freight transfer. A single job may include moving a thousand pieces of valuable office equipment and furniture and entail supervising a crew of up to sixty for two twelve-hour shifts around the clock over the course of several days. No big deal for John.

"The business is based on problem solving," says John. "If I have to put the guys up in a hotel to get the job done, I'll do it. That's how it works. You have to stay committed."

His commitment earned revenues of $500,000 in 1998, and John has garnered the trust and respect of some of the biggest companies in the Washington, D.C., area. He has counted among his accounts US Airways, State Farm Insurance Company, and Metropolitan Life Insurance Company. Over the course of fifteen years, John has built a reputation that keeps him in demand.

"The perfect move is when a client says, 'Here's the blueprint. Move it, and call us when you're done,'" John says. "We can do that."

Not only do companies seeking his services keep him busy; so do other movers who lack the manpower for a big job.

"We're so good that all the big moving companies want to work with us," says John, thirty-seven, adding that even companies who bid against him for jobs never deride Logan Transfer because they never know when they'll have to call on him. "If they win the bid and don't have enough capacity to do the job, we're there."

Things are great compared to what it was like for John starting out as a commercial mover in 1985. On one of the first contracts he won, he discovered the importance of being able to trust the people with whom he works as well as his capacity to do whatever is necessary to get the job done.

In the Beginning

"I busted my butt in the beginning. I once had a four-man job, and three guys didn't show up. I did it myself," recalls John. "But I did heroic stuff like that because I didn't have a choice."

Logan Transfer is actually an outgrowth of a courier business John started when he was looking for something to do. A native of Washington, D.C., his family moved to suburban Kensington, Maryland, where he graduated from high school. He went to college at Central State University in Ohio and majored in business administration. Although he was a good student, he was restless and dropped out after a couple of years. He returned to Washington and took a job helping companies register their cellular phone businesses with the Federal Communications Commission. It was less a job than a party. He was twenty years old and worked with a bunch of guys around the same age and for a boss who wasn't much older. They spent a number of afternoons hanging out and drinking beer.

"It was like working in a frat house," laughs John.

The goofing off finally took its toll, and John was fired. He wasn't concerned about leaving the FCC job because he had never really been comfortable in the traditional corporate-government atmosphere. He *was* concerned about paying his bills. When the gas, electric, and telephone services were cut off in his apartment, he moved home and started serious job hunting. He ended up working for a courier service and taking classes at the University of the District of Columbia, and life was actually pretty good for a twenty-year-old kid. John didn't have to be at work until 1 P.M., and he was assigned mainly to a company called Ankers Photographers, an old, established firm that did a lot of work for congressmen and senators on Capitol Hill. John would pick up packets of photos and deliver them all over The Hill. He grew to like the proprietors and observed that the courier company for which he worked was making a killing. It occurred to him one day to ask whether Ankers would be interested in cutting out the middleman and hiring John to do all their courier work.

"I didn't know what a business was, but I asked the woman at Ankers, and she said yes," says John, who also remembers that he didn't even know how to write out an invoice.

"When it was time to get paid, I asked for a check, and she said I needed to give her a bill," he says. "So I wrote something on a piece of paper, and she wrote me a check. I was in business."

That was in 1982, and he worked three hours a day, making $250 a week. John named his company American Courier Service and stayed in business for three years, taking the occasional part-time job to supplement his income. But that was decent money for what he was doing, and he was happy to drift along until he got married.

"I wanted to do the male responsibility thing and take care of my family," says John. "So I started knocking on doors to see what would happen next."

He started with freight and furniture companies, where work was easy to get. He was willing to learn and in a sense grew up with his business.

"I got skilled at moving furniture—which does involve some skill," says John. "It's important to be meticulous, quick, and careful. On occasion, I'd have to hire people, so I started to develop management skills. I became responsible, and I was doing it my way without having to climb the corporate ladder."

> *J*ohn believes in second chances, and he believes in a supportive and empowering work environment.

He bought one ramshackle truck financed with savings and his pick-up work. It broke down as often as it ran. But John would climb underneath, fix it, and then go on to the next job. He developed a reputation for reliability in word and deed. After a year he had two trucks, then four, and four guys working for him.

He is respected inside as well as outside his company. John likes to hire men who have a tough time getting jobs anywhere else, men with personal problems and some with criminal records. But he believes in second chances, and he believes in a supportive and empowering work environment.

"I like to encourage people to recognize that there is another way to get through life, that there is a good path."

John is willing to teach anyone who wants to learn about the commercial moving business, and he gives his supervisors more and more responsibility with less oversight as they gain expertise, making his employees and contract workers feel that he trusts their judgment and that they are capable of making important decisions.

"All my guys respect me," says John. And he feels the same way—he respects them. "They take me seriously because I know what I'm doing, and I really care about my employees. I want that to trickle down."

He informs his management style with patience—John is above everything a laid-back guy—and tries hard to be "clear and fair."

Above all, John likes what he does, and he appreciates the fact that he has succeeded on his own terms.

Index